THE MURDER OF
KING TUT

Also by James Patterson

For more information about James Patterson's novels, visit
www.jamespatterson.co.uk

James Patterson
& Martin Dugard
THE MURDER OF
KING TUT

Century · London

Published by Century, 2009

4 6 8 10 9 7 5 3

Copyright © James Patterson, 2009
Illustrated maps © Scott Murphy, 2009

James Patterson has asserted his right under the Copyright, Designs
and Patents Act 1988 to be identified as the author of this work.

First published in Great Britain in 2009 by
Century
Random House, 20 Vauxhall Bridge Road,
London SW1V 2SA

www.randomhouse.co.uk

Addresses for companies within The Random House Group Limited can be found at:
www.randomhouse.co.uk/offices.htm

The Random House Group Limited Reg. No. 954009

A CIP catalogue record for this book
is available from the British Library

Hardback ISBN: 9781846055171
Trade paperback ISBN: 9781846055188

The Random House Group Limited supports The Forest Stewardship
Council (FSC), the leading international forest certification organisation. All our
titles that are printed on Greenpeace approved FSC certified paper carry the
FSC logo. Our paper procurement policy can be found at:
www.rbooks.co.uk/environment

Mixed Sources
Product group from well-managed
forests and other controlled sources
www.fsc.org Cert no. TT-COC-2139
© 1996 Forest Stewardship Council
FSC

Printed and bound in Great Britain by
Clays Ltd, St Ives plc

For Frank Nicolo
—JP

For Callie
—MD

Author's Note

JUST LIKE THE ASSOCIATED PRESS, I have my own style manual. "JP Writing Style and Book Elements" is a list of nineteen bulleted points that I keep within arm's reach whenever I'm working. Point number eighteen is written in capital letters, because no matter how often I read it, I need to be reminded that it is of the utmost importance: RESEARCH HELPS. DON'T FAKE ANYTHING—NOT BRAIN TUMORS, NOT DROWN-INGS, NOT EVEN A BEE STING.

I don't think I've ever done more research for a book. From the instant the idea hit me and I teamed up with Marty Dugard to write this story, it's been total immersion in ancient Egypt. The book is a murder mystery, but the plunge back in time added a whole other layer of detective work. We didn't just need to know the players in our drama; we also needed to know what foods they ate, the clothes they wore, how they loved, and, ultimately, the ways they might have killed each other.

Like number eighteen says: DON'T FAKE ANYTHING.

So we didn't. Marty's historical legwork involved trips to London and to Tut's tomb in Egypt's Valley of the Kings. I lost myself in books and online research. We then combined our notes and began writing. One astounding fact about Egyptian history is that so much of it is still unknown. So when we came to a gap, we went back to the research for answers. Then we put forth our theory as to what happened. We constructed conversations and motives and rich scenes of palace life—all grounded in long hours of research.

It's nothing new for histories to be speculative, but there's a difference between guessing and basing a theory on cold hard facts. We chose the facts.

As for Howard Carter, he is almost a contemporary, so his life was much easier to document. I resisted the temptation to speculate about his relationship with Lady Evelyn Herbert, though I thoroughly hoped to find a steamy journal entry that would allow me to muse at will. You can draw your own conclusions.

Author's Note

I hope you enjoy *The Murder of King Tut*. It's been a lot of fun to write. I became quite fond of the ill-fated boy pharaoh and his equally ill-fated queen. They lived thousands of years ago, but their love for each other was so powerful and real that I believe they had one of history's great romances. It's a shame it all had to end so soon — and so mysteriously.

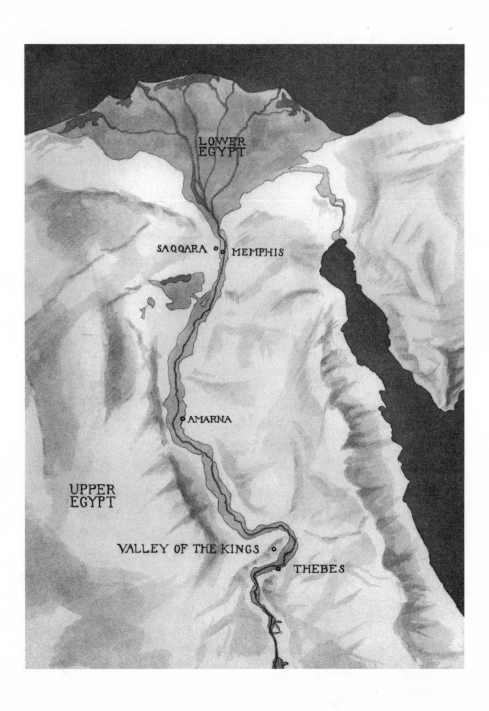

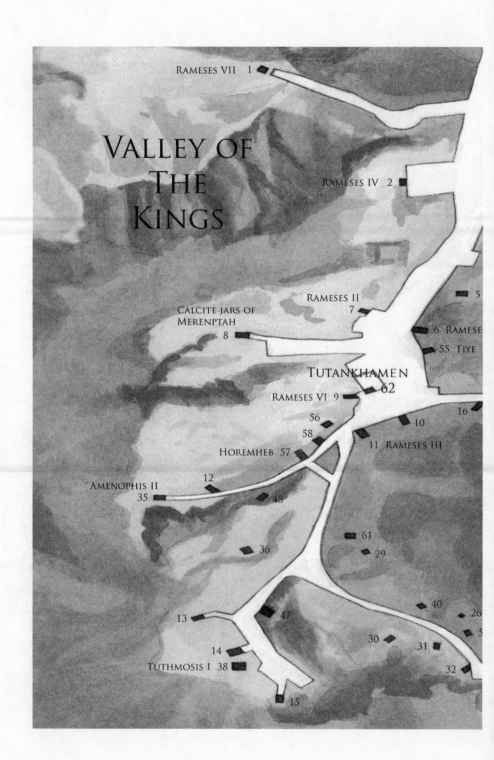

RAMESES VII 1

RAMESES IV 2

VALLEY OF
THE
KINGS

RAMESES II
7

5

Calcite jars of
Merenptah
8

6 RAMESE

55 TIYE

TUTANKHAMEN
62

RAMESES VI 9

56

16

58

10

HOREMHEB 57

11 RAMESES III

12

AMENOPHIS II
35

48

61

36

29

40

26

13

47

30

31

5

14

TUTHMOSIS I 38

32

15

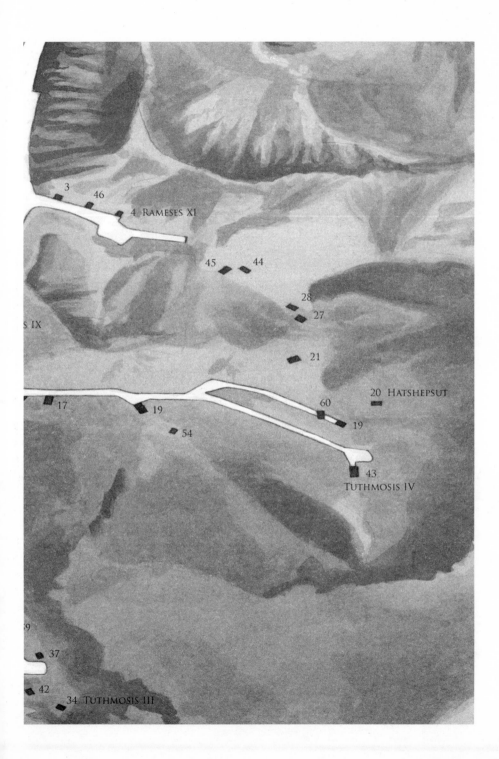

3
46
4 RAMESES XI
45
44
28
27
S IX
21
17
19
20 HATSHEPSUT
60
19
54
43
TUTHMOSIS IV
9
37
42
34 TUTHMOSIS III

Prologue

Valley of the Kings
1900

IT WAS NEW YEAR'S EVE as a somber, good-looking explorer named Howard Carter, speaking fluent Arabic, gave the order to begin digging.

Carter stood in a claustrophobic chamber more than three hundred feet underground. The air was dank, but he craved a cigarette. He was addicted to the damn things. Sweat rings stained the armpits of his white button-down, and dust coated his work boots. The sandal-clad Egyptian workers at his side began to shovel for all they were worth.

It had been almost two years since Carter had been

thrown from his horse far out in the desert. That lucky fall had changed his life.

He had landed hard on the stony soil but was amazed to find himself peering at a deep cleft in the ground. It appeared to be the hidden entrance to an ancient burial chamber.

Working quickly and in secret, the twenty-six-year-old Egyptologist obtained the proper government permissions, then hired a crew to begin digging.

Now he expected to become famous at a very young age—and filthy rich.

Early-Egyptian rulers had been buried inside elaborate stone pyramids, but centuries of ransacking by tomb robbers inspired later pharaohs to conceal their burial sites by carving them into the ground.

Once a pharaoh died, was mummified, and then sealed inside such a tomb with all his worldly possessions, great pains were taken to hide its location.

But that didn't help. Tomb robbers seemed to find every one.

Carter, a square-shouldered man who favored bow ties, linen trousers, and homburg hats, thought this tomb might be the exception. The limestone chips that had been dumped into the tunnels and shaft by some long-ago builder—a simple yet ingenious method to keep out bandits—appeared untouched.

Carter and his workers had already spent months removing the shards. With each load that was hauled away, he became more and more certain that there was a great undisturbed burial chamber hidden deep within the ground. If he was right, the tomb would be filled with priceless treasures: gold and gems, as well as a pharaoh's mummy.

Howard Carter would be rich beyond his wildest dreams, and his dreams were indeed spectacular.

"The men have now gone down ninety-seven meters vertical drop," Carter had written to Lady Amherst, his longtime patron, "and still no end." Indeed, when widened the narrow opening that he had stumbled upon revealed a network of tunnels leading farther underground.

At one point, a tunnel branched off into a chamber, that contained a larger-than-life statue of an Egyptian pharaoh.

But that tunnel had dead-ended into a vertical shaft filled with rock and debris.

As the months passed, the workers forged on, digging ever deeper, so deep in fact that the men had to be lowered down by rope each day. Carter's hopes soared. He even took the unusual step of contacting Britain's consul general in Cairo to prepare him for the glorious moment when a "virgin" tomb would be opened.

Now he stood at the bottom of the shaft. Before him was a doorway sealed with plaster and stamped with the mark of a pharaoh—*the entrance to a burial chamber.*

Carter ordered his workers to knock it down.

The shaft was suddenly choked with noise and a storm of dust as the men used picks and crowbars to demolish the ancient door. Carter hacked into his handkerchief as he struggled to see through the haze.

His heart raced as he finally held his lantern into the burial chamber. The workers standing behind him peered excitedly over his shoulder.

There was nothing there.

The treasure, and the pharaoh's mummy, had already been stolen.

By somebody else.

Palm Beach, Florida
Present Day

"THIS IS JAMES PATTERSON CALLING. Is Michael around? I have a mystery story to tell him."

As most people would expect, I love a good mystery, and I thought I might have unearthed a real doozy to write about, which was why I had put in a call to my editor at Little, Brown, Michael Pietsch, who is also the publisher.

As I waited for Michael to come on the line— he usually takes my calls, night or day—I looked around my second-floor office. *Am I completely mad?* I wondered.

The last thing I needed right now was another

writing project. I already had a new Alex Cross novel on the fires, and a Women's Murder Club brewing, and a Maximum Ride to finish. In fact, there were *twenty-four* manuscripts—none of them yet completed—laid out on the expansive desk surface that occupies most of my office. I could read some of the titles: *Swimsuit, Witch & Wizard, Daniel X, Women's Murder Club 9, Worst Case...*

"I *am* completely crazy, aren't I?" I said as Pietsch came on the line. Michael is a calm and calming presence, very smart, and a wonderful father who knows how to handle children—like me—most of the time. Over the years we have become a good fit and have turned out more than a dozen number one bestsellers together.

"Of course you're crazy, but why the phone call?" he asked. "Why aren't you writing?"

"I have an idea."

"Only one?"

"I really like this one, Michael. Let me talk at you for a minute. OK? Since you seem to know everything about everything, you are probably aware that a collection of King Tut memorabilia is touring the world. People are lining up everywhere; the exhibit is usually sold out weeks in advance. I actually visited a Tut exhibit years ago at the Met in New York, and then recently in Fort Lauderdale. I've seen firsthand how Tut's story blows people's minds—men, women and children, rich and poor.

"There's something about Tut that brings ancient Egypt to life for most of us. It's not just the incredible treasures he was buried with, or the art, or the near-miraculous discovery of the burial chamber by Howard Carter. It's all of that, of course, but there's something magical here, something iconic. Tut's name was scrubbed from Egyptian history books for thousands of years, and now Tut is probably the most famous pharaoh of them all. *And yet nobody knows that much about him.*

"Michael, I want to do a book about Tut. Three parts: present day, as I learn—*hopefully*—more and more about the boy king; then the amazing discovery of the tomb and treasures by Carter, who is probably worth a book on his own; and a third part about Tut himself.

"Did you know that Tut married his *sister*—and that theirs was an incredible love story? So what do you think? Are you going to try to stop me? Just this once, will you save me from myself?"

Michael's infectious laughter traveled across the phone lines. "How's the new Alex Cross coming?" he asked.

"Almost done—ahead of schedule. You're going to like it."

"Well, Jim, like just about everyone else, I'm fascinated by ancient Egypt, the pyramids, the Valley of the Kings, Tut, Nefertiti, the Rameses boys. So I have to tell you, I like the idea very much."

Now it was my turn to smile and to laugh in relief.

"I'm really glad. So let me tell you what I thought would close the deal—though, obviously, I don't need it. Michael, I have a hunch that Tut was murdered. And I hope, at least on paper, to prove it."

Michael laughed again. "You had me at 'King Tut,'" he quipped.

Part One

Chapter 1

Valley of the Kings
1492 BC

"THIS IS FAR ENOUGH! Stop right here."

More than five hundred prisoners of war halted their march toward Thebes in a great field situated two miles from the city. A contingent of the palace guard watched over them in the sweltering midday sun. Not that it was necessary. The emaciated prisoners' feet were bound with leather cord that was just long enough for them to frog walk; they could not run.

And even if they had tried to escape, their arms were tied behind their backs at the wrist and elbow.

They wouldn't get far, and the punishment would be swift and brutal.

Ineni, the well-regarded royal architect, watched over the sad scene. He knew these men well. They had just spent five years in a remote valley, excavating a new burial place for Tuthmosis I.

By day they had endured withering summer heat and surprisingly frigid blasts of desert cold that sometimes strafed the valley.

At night they had slept under a sky shot through with stars.

It had been more than a thousand years since Cheops had built his great pyramid up the Nile in Giza. As grand and awe-inspiring as they were, pyramids turned out to be beacons of temptation for every local thief and blasphemous tomb robber. There wasn't a single one that hadn't been looted. Not one.

But the ingenious Ineni believed he had the solution to the pyramid problem. Using the slave labor provided by these prisoners, he had carved a *secret* burial chamber for Tuthmosis I. The aging pharaoh was sick and near death, so the timing of the tomb's completion was perfect. Not merely a makeshift cave, the tomb contained several tunnels, hallways, and a half dozen rooms. The pharaoh's stone sarcophagus would reside precisely in the center, in the largest, most luxurious room.

True, Ineni thought, brushing a bead of sweat from his eyebrow, *such an underground tomb was hardly as grand as a soaring pyramid. But in many ways it was better.* The walls were smooth to the touch and painted with vivid scenes from the pharaoh's life—both the one he had just lived and the glorious one yet to come.

Most important, the pharaoh would be undisturbed. Hopefully, for all eternity. At least that was what most Egyptians believed happened when a pharaoh was put to rest.

Ineni liked the design so much that he was already working on a similar tomb for himself. "I superintended the excavations of the cliff tomb of His Majesty," Ineni had written on the walls of his own burial chamber—it was the architect's way of bragging to those in the afterworld—"Alone, no one seeing, no one hearing."

Of course, he hadn't been totally alone. The prisoners had done their part. He had gotten to know them, Hittites and Nubians. He'd heard about their wives and children and knew that the men cherished their families with the same passion that he loved his. Some of the prisoners had become his friends.

After the tomb for Tuthmosis I was sealed and the entry concealed with stone, he had marched the men away from the area—a place that one day would simply be known as the Valley of the Kings, because so many other pharaohs would choose Ineni's architectural contrivance as a means of hiding their final resting places.

Ineni scanned the faces of the prisoners. They knew the location of the pharaoh's secret tomb, and that was unacceptable. The architect turned away from the men, then signaled to the guards.

"Do what must be done. Be merciful. Do it quickly. These are good men."

And so the bloody slaughter of the prisoners began. Their screams rose to the heavens, and Ineni hoped that the many gods of Egypt approved of his difficult but necessary decision.

Chapter 2

Thebes
1357 BC

AMENHOTEP THE MAGNIFICENT knocked back a stiff jolt of red wine as he shuffled into the sunlit throne room.

Once upon a time the pharaoh had been lean and muscular, a warrior feared throughout the known world. He was also said to have had sexual relations with more than five hundred consorts and concubines.

Now he was "prosperous," which was a polite way of saying that his great belly preceded him wherever he went.

"You'll get fat from all that wine," cooed Tiye, his

queen and favorite wife — possibly because she had a sense of humor that matched his own.

"Too late." Amenhotep slurred his words noticeably. "At least a dozen years too late."

Just back from a morning of sailing, Tiye had entered from the main hall without fanfare, her sandaled feet quietly slapping the tile floor. The queen had full lips, a pleasingly ample bosom, and wore a white linen dress with vertical blue stripes that was cinched at her narrow waist.

They both knew why she'd come to see him today.

"Pharaoh," she said, standing over him, "we must talk. This one time you must listen to a woman, my love. You *must*."

Amenhotep pretended to ignore his queen. He thought about swabbing a little opium on his abscessed teeth, just to take the edge off, and then maybe having a nap before dinner. No. First a visit to the lovely Resi over at the harem for a midafternoon romp, then sleep. Resi had an even larger bosom than Tiye, and she was a better actress in bed. Amenhotep got a happy feeling just thinking about the whore.

Up in Memphis, the northern capital of his kingdom, the bureaucrats would be pestering him with crop reports and tax estimates. Nothing but meetings all day long. Yes, Egypt needed officials like that; the country would be a lawless backwater without the legion of clerks. But after three decades in power, Amenhotep needed a break.

Which is why he loved Thebes much more than Memphis.

Thebes, just a week's journey up the Nile from Memphis, was so different than the northern capital, it might as well have been in a separate country. In Thebes a pharaoh could bask for hours in the desert sun, drink wine whenever he wanted, and make love to his entire harem—a dozen beauties, each selected by him—without a single bureaucratic interruption. In Thebes a pharaoh had time to think, to dream. In Thebes the pharaoh answered to no one—except his wife.

Amenhotep looked up at Tiye. "I am a fat old pharaoh who is no longer fit to rule this kingdom. Is that what you're about to say? I am a whoremaster without a conscience? What am I? Tell me."

Tiye bit her tongue. In many ways, she loved this fat old man, this *deity*. But now Amenhotep was dying. Decisions had to be made before it was too late—for Egypt, and for its queen.

"All right," he sighed. "Let's talk. I'm dying. What of it?"

Chapter 3

Thebes
1357 BC

"THE FUTURE OF EGYPT is at stake. You know that. You need to take action."

"I will never share power with *that accident*," shouted the pharaoh.

Amenhotep had rallied somewhat from his drunken state. Now the palace walls shook with his angry protestations. He and Tiye were alone, but everyone from the bodyguards at the door to the servant girls polishing the great tiled hallway were privy to their battle. Soon these commoners would be gossiping to their friends and families, and the details of the royal argument would spread throughout Thebes.

"You are speaking about *a child* created in a moment of passion. Perhaps the pharaoh would like to describe what was accidental about that."

"I do not regret the act of making love, only the result of our lovemaking. He will not reign as co-regent. I couldn't bear it. He is a sniveling whelp."

Tiye sneered. "We both know that he will succeed you one day."

"You hope so, don't you? Does my queen not admit that she has selfish reasons for wanting that boy elevated to co-regent?"

"The queen admits nothing of the kind. The queen wants what's best for Egypt. Surely you wish your son to step into power—armed with your many years of hard-earned wisdom?"

You will lose everything if someone else succeeds me, thought a cynical Amenhotep. *So don't tell me what's best for Egypt. Have you braved thirst and burning deserts to wage war on the Hittites? Have you smelled the cedar forests of Byblos? You wear the gold and lapis lazuli that come as tribute from lands I conquered, but you know nothing of the world outside Thebes.*

"His arms hang to his knees, and his face is as long as a horse's," Amenhotep declared. "He hasn't enough muscle to wield a sword. His only muscles are in his head. To be pharaoh is to be god in the flesh. That boy is a freak."

"He was born to lead our people. He can drive a

chariot as well as any man," said Tiye. "He is well read and smart."

The pharaoh snorted. The mere sight of his son—also named Amenhotep—at the reins of a chariot was hilarious. It was a wonder the imbecile hadn't been trampled to death already. "Steering through a grain field is one thing. Charging into battle is quite another," he said.

Suddenly, Amenhotep felt woozy. The opium had gone to work, but the pain was still unbearable. What he needed was more wine. And Resi's bosom to suck on.

Amenhotep ignored his goblet and raised the full pitcher to his lips. The ruby liquid spilled along his face, then trickled down his thick neck and under his collar onto the copper skin of his belly. It came to rest on the white kilt around his waist, leaving a stain that looked like blood.

The pharaoh tumbled backward into his pillows. This was an act of retreat, and they both knew it.

Tiye stood over him to close the deal, as the sun's fiery rays taunted the crocodiles and cobras painted on the tile floor. "This must be done, pharaoh. And soon."

"They are almost finished decorating my burial chamber," the pharaoh muttered. He reached for a plate of bread flavored with honey and dates, unaware that the grains of sand in every bite were the source of his pain. Year after year, the desert grit in the bread wore away the enamel on his teeth, inviting the decay and infection that would soon take his life.

Tiye handed him another goblet filled to the brim with wine, then remained still as Amenhotep chased the bread with a long gulp. She was as serene as the Sphinx as she waited for her husband to bend to her strong will.

"Tuthmosis would have been a great pharaoh," he said mournfully.

"That son now wanders the afterworld," Tiye replied.

Amenhotep nodded sadly. Their oldest boy, his beloved, his favorite, was dead. Soon he would join him. Egypt would need a new pharaoh. The only way to control the selection was to do it himself.

"Bring the accident to me," Amenhotep roared. "Of course he will be pharaoh. But shame on me for leaving Egypt to him. Shame on both of us."

Chapter 4

Didlington Hall
near Swaffham, England
1887

"HOWARD, IS THAT YOU? What do you think you're doing in here?" asked Lord Amherst, swinging open the library doors. "These artifacts are *irreplaceable*. I've told you that before. You are a stubborn boy."

Thirteen-year-old Howard Carter quickly turned his head toward His Lordship. He was caught! He had been warned repeatedly about this room. He was definitely a stubborn boy.

It was the middle of the day. Young Carter was supposed to be helping his father, who was painting a new commission for His Lordship. In a moment of boredom, the boy had slipped away to the most for-

24

bidden and imposing room at Didlington Hall: *the library*.

He couldn't help himself. The room was utterly fascinating, its silence augmented by the startling, massive stone statues situated about the room, imported straight from the sands of Egypt. To gaze at them allowed Carter to see into the history of the known world. These pieces truly *were* irreplaceable.

Didlington Hall was a palatial fortress eight miles south of Swaffham. It was the county seat of Lord Amherst, a member of parliament with a penchant for styling his hair in the foppish manner of Oscar Wilde. Seven thousand acres and sixteen leased farms surrounded the great home. There was a large, pristine lake, a paddock, a falconer's lodge, a boat house, and a ballroom that had been host to grand and important parties for more than a hundred years.

But it was the library that Howard Carter loved most, and he couldn't stay out of the room.

Fortunately, Lord Amherst was a nice man with five daughters; Carter was the closest thing to a son he'd ever had. He recognized the slender, strong-jawed young man's innate, sometimes fierce curiosity and saw something of himself in him.

He and young Carter both wanted — no, that would be too soft a description — *demanded* answers about what had come before them. They were obsessed with the ancient past.

So rather than kicking Carter out of the library, Lord Amherst proceeded to walk him through the wood-paneled room, patiently explaining the significance of the more notable books.

There was a priceless collection of Bibles for example, many printed centuries earlier. There was a section devoted to *incunabula*, books printed shortly after the invention of the printing press. There were books with fancy bindings, first editions by famous authors, and so forth and so on.

And then there was the *Egyptian* collection.

In addition to owning tome after tome detailing the known history of ancient Egypt, Lord Amherst had rather obsessively decorated the library with Egyptian relics. The taller statues were bigger than a man and loomed like sentinels among the overstuffed wingback chairs and oil reading lamps. There were dozens of smaller statues too, and rare texts printed on papyrus that had been sealed behind glass so human hands like Howard's couldn't damage them. Amherst had bought the collection from a German priest two decades earlier and had added to it every year since.

"Not only is it the largest collection of Egyptology in all of Great Britain," he told Carter, "it is the joy of my life."

"And mine as well," Carter chimed in.

The tour concluded with a history-changing announcement: Lord Amherst was hereby offering the young man unlimited access to his collection. Never mind that something as simple as bumping into a statue could cause thousands of pounds' worth of damage— Amherst had seen the passion in Carter's eyes as he told him of the mysteries of Egyptian culture, with its strange alphabet and belief in the afterworld and the amazing burial chambers.

Amherst encouraged Carter to immerse himself in Egyptology. And that was precisely what Howard Carter did—until the day he died.

Chapter 5

Didlington Hall
1891

IT WAS LATE MAY, almost June. Howard Carter, now seventeen, strode up the Watteau Walk toward the white columns marking the south entrance of Didlington Hall.

There was a fragrance of fresh grass in the air but a weariness in his step. He had spent the day as he spent most every other day, sketching household pets. It was a living—not a good living, and certainly not an exciting living, but he had no other skills and little formal education. Though he had grown accustomed to being treated as family by the Amhersts, the fact of the matter was that while he could put on airs with the best of the nobility and was always welcome to spend hours in Lord Amherst's library, he was doomed to a life of very modest income and minimal prestige.

He simply had to accept the fact that he would be a nobody, accomplishing nothing. But it made him grumpy. Very much so.

Chapter 6

Didlington Hall
1891

CARTER STEPPED into the cool entryway. This was much better. The great expanse was lined with expensive paintings and other works of art, some of which dated to the eleventh century.

A butler showed Carter to the library.

Lady Amherst was there, as was her youngest, twenty-five-year-old Alicia. They greeted Carter warmly and introduced him to an affable stranger who clearly had a flirtatious relationship with Alicia. Carter didn't much like that, but what Alicia did wasn't his concern.

The stranger was a bony young man in his early

twenties named Perky Newberry. His face and hands were deeply tanned from hours outdoors, and his face was half covered with a prominent mustache.

Carter soon learned that Newberry was an Egyptologist who was pursuing Alicia's heart and Lady Amherst's pocketbook. He was fresh from a November–April stint along the Nile, surveying ruins at a place called Beni Hasan.

Lady Amherst, who had always loved Carter, was obviously keen on having the two of them meet. He wasn't sure why.

But Carter sat and listened eagerly as Newberry told incredible stories about life on the Nile. He spoke of working in the tombs from first light all the way through to the evening meal, then devoting the greater part of the night to study and discussion. Newberry's tone was intense, and he had a deep passion for his work. Carter liked him instantly.

It also turned out that Perky was something of a botanist, which seemed a rather unusual sideline for a man laboring in such a barren location. But Carter remembered that Alicia also enjoyed botany, and then their connection made sense.

On behalf of the British Museum, Newberry's expedition had undertaken to create a visual record of the drawings and colorful hieroglyphics inside the pharaohs' tombs before they completely faded away—something that often happened when ancient drawings were exposed to air and the presence of human beings. The task was enormous. There were some *twelve thousand square feet* of wall drawings to sketch.

And while the job had gone well at first, the relationship between Newberry and his sketch artist had soured. Now, as he was raising money to fund another season in Egypt, Newberry was also searching for a new sketch artist. The job required someone with significant knowledge of Egypt and a talent for drawing and painting.

That person, it soon became obvious, was Howard Carter.

Chapter 7

Alexandria
1891

ONLY THE HUGELY IRRITATING FACT that he was seasick prevented Carter from bursting with excitement. My God, he was in Alexandria, Egypt. He steadied himself against the roll of the steamship as he scanned the docks for Perky Newberry.

Carter had just reached the ancient port founded by Alexander the Great, the man responsible for *ending* the great Egyptian empires. Some said the city was the gateway to Africa; others called it the crossroads of the world. For the seventeen-year-old Carter, Alexandria was simply the place where his life would begin, the life he believed he had been born for.

But first he had to find Perky Newberry.

It was Newberry who had rescued Carter from the tedium of drawing family pets and had sent him to train at the British Museum so he would be prepared for his role as a sketch artist.

Perky had gone ahead of Carter to Egypt and now should have been waiting for him on shore.

Somewhere. *But where?*

Carter was slender, with a lantern jaw and a whisper of the bushy mustache he would wear for the next four decades. The air was hot like the mouth of a blast furnace, and he could feel the searing heat of the deck burning through the soles of his shoes.

He was dressed for October in England, not October in Egypt. He would have eagerly traded his suit and tie for the dockworkers' simple white robes. None of them seemed bothered by the heat.

Carter squinted into the pale sunshine, scanning the distant dock for a sign of Newberry. But there was no Englishman among the mélange of half-dressed Moors, Turks, Nubians, and Egyptians. No sign of Newberry's straw hat.

Where in hell are you, Perky?

Carter studied the skyline and spotted Pompey's priapic pillar jutting above Alexandria like some ancient Roman practical joke.

He double-checked that he had everything he

needed to go ashore. His list was short: sketchbook, notebook, valise.

The ship's anchors splashed into the Great Harbor like a shotgun blast. Immediately, a locust-like plague of dockworkers clambered up over the side.

Carter barely avoided being knocked over as he made his way to the gangplank being lowered off the edge of the ship. He scuttled down into a waiting boat, where a local man whose rippling shoulders told of years of plying the harbor rowed him ashore.

Carter paid the man and stepped up onto the stone dock. And there stood Perky Newberry, resplendent in his straw boater, smiling broadly.

"Where were you?" Carter dared to complain to his boss and employer. "I'm always prompt and efficient myself."

Perky Newberry just laughed. "Well, you'd better be, with that attitude of yours. Welcome to Egypt, Carter."

Howard Carter's Egyptian adventure was about to begin. Though he didn't realize it then, a boy had come to find the boy king.

Chapter 8

Beni Hasan

1891

CARTER WOKE UP INSIDE A TOMB. He was eager to begin working, though it was totally dark, and the small room smelled like, well, death warmed over.

The floor of the burial place was carved stone covered in a fine layer of sand. Bats clung to the ceiling, the rustle of their wings making a sound like what Carter would one day call "strange spirits of the ancient dead."

Newberry lay nearby. Like Carter, he had spent the night in the tomb, for they had arrived after nightfall and had nowhere else to sleep.

If this was to be Howard Carter's first day as an

Egyptologist — and it was — it couldn't have gotten off to a more atmospheric start.

From Alexandria, Carter and Newberry had taken the train to Cairo, where they spent a week with Flinders Petrie, whom Lord Amherst had called "the master" of Egyptian excavation for his years of experience in the tombs.

Those days spent in the Egyptian metropolis had been exciting, but soon it was time to move on. From Cairo, Carter and Newberry chugged south.

The tracks hugged the Nile, but while the scenery on the train ride from Alexandria had been lush and green through the river delta, just outside Cairo it had turned barren and desolate. A thin strip of greenery sprouted along either side of the Nile, thanks to its annual habit of overflowing its banks, but otherwise the sensation of being surrounded by desert was powerful indeed.

After two hundred miles, the men disembarked at Abu Qirqas station, where they hired donkeys — one each for themselves, and one each for their luggage.

Carter had no problem handling his animals, thanks to his many years living in the country.

"Just watch me," he told Perky Newberry. "Do as I do, and you'll be fine."

The fertile black loam of the riverside path soon turned dry and rocky. The sun was setting, and Carter and Newberry knew that it would be a race just to get to the tombs before dark.

They lost.

The trail became increasingly narrow and rugged as it climbed an escarpment. But eventually they reached the tombs, which provided acceptable shelter from the wind and nighttime cold. Their remote location allowed the two men to simply step through the ancient stone doorway and stretch out for the night.

Now Carter shuffled outside to see for himself what the Egyptian desert looked like at dawn. He wasn't disappointed.

"The view was breathtaking," he later wrote in his schoolboy prose style. "The Nile Valley glowing softly in the sunlight, stretching far into the distance, the edges of the tawny desert contrasting amiably with the fertile plain."

He was in a land that couldn't have been more different from the verdant pastures of Swaffham.

But Howard Carter felt like he had finally come home.

Chapter 9

Thebes
1347 BC

THE MAD ROAR OF THE CROWD penetrated the temple's thick stone walls, shaking them to their foundations. It was bedlam of the most unnerving sort on the streets of Thebes—deafening noise mingled with the spectacle of men and women frantically making love in back alleys, oblivious to the stench of stale urine, desert dust, and whiskey vomit.

Such was the Sed festival in Thebes, a time when all of Egypt celebrated the immortality of the pharaoh. But the partying was happening on the other side of these sacred walls.

Inside the temple at Karnak, Queen Nefertiti

was oblivious to the noise of the masses. A slender, shaven-headed package of genius and raw sexuality, she had the habit of making men weak in the knees by her mere presence. (Her name means "a beautiful woman has come.") Nefertiti was also known for her poise, but at the moment she was seized by an urge to slap someone hard across the face.

Whether it should be her anxious wimp of a husband or the silly sculptor with the peasant beard who was taking hours to draw a simple sketch, she couldn't decide.

So Nefertiti settled onto her throne and tried to see her husband through the eyes of the sculptor. Amenhotep IV was in his early twenties and at the height of his power and virility. Yet he had generous hips and the breasts of a woman, as well as hideous buck teeth and long spidery hands. *And those ears! Could they possibly get any bigger?*

Yet she loved him in her way. All his life, her husband had been a freak. But he was her freak, and that freak happened to be the pharaoh, which made her queen.

And what a queen she was turning out to be — performing sacred rituals once reserved just for pharaohs; frequently wearing the Nubian wig that only men had worn prior; even driving her own chariot with the skill of a man.

Much of this was possible because Egypt had

always treated women better than other ancient civilizations had. Women could conduct business, own property, represent themselves in legal disputes, study and become doctors. Women had even become pharaoh, and queens with the strength of Nefertiti could control their much weaker husbands.

"You look divine," purred Nefertiti now, though it was she who felt beautiful. The sheer white gown, floral headdress, and priceless golden amulets decorating her arms accentuated her physical attributes and radiance. The makeup, which she and the pharaoh both wore, did more for him than it did for her.

"I *am* divine," laughed Amenhotep IV. It was their little joke.

"Is it so difficult to show me as I am?" he finally barked at the artist. He was a new pharaoh and still didn't understand that raising his voice showed weakness. His father, Amenhotep the Magnificent, had died from a painful infection of the mouth. Now Amenhotep IV, who had briefly served alongside his father as co-regent, stood to flick a bee off his shaved chest.

He missed.

Nefertiti stepped forward and brushed away the bee before it could sting him, then held her husband's hand. She saw that he looked all too human on this, the day Egypt was supposed to bask in his strength as pharaoh.

This was a problem: The pharaoh needed to prove his immortality by galloping a chariot through the teeming masses outside. Even under the best of conditions, it was a bold and reckless ride that could easily end in a crash, which would be a disaster for the young pharaoh.

As palace insiders were all too aware, Amenhotep IV was very poor at the reins of a chariot. This ritual race could become a suicide run for him.

Yet if by some miracle he pulled it off, his claim to Egypt's throne would be secure. No longer would his masculinity be questioned. With one death-defying ride, Amenhotep IV would demonstrate his power in a most public way. Egypt would know that he was their one true pharaoh.

But if anything went wrong—if Amenhotep IV got thrown or dropped the reins and crashed into the crowd; if a wheel somehow broke off, and the chariot spun out of control—it would be obvious that the strange-looking man claiming to be the pharaoh was no god. And if a pharaoh was not divine, the temple high priests would find another to take his place.

Somehow they would kill him. And possibly his queen as well.

"How are you?" Nefertiti asked. "I have nothing but confidence in you, sire."

"You lie—so beautifully," the pharaoh replied.

"How much longer?" Nefertiti whirled and shouted at the sculptor.

"At least thirty minutes." The callous little man crumpled a sheet of papyrus to start fresh.

"You have *ten*."

"But Queen—"

"Not a second more."

"I'll do my best," the sculptor replied.

Nefertiti pursed her lips in a thin crocodile smile—and made a mental note to have the so-called artist killed once the statue was complete.

Chapter 10

Thebes
1347 BC

THE PRIESTS, PREENING AND PRATTLING, filed into the temple room when the sculptor finally left. They were as haughty as the queen's famed cats. Nefertiti despised their power and how they used religion to make themselves rich. Indeed, Ptahmose, the high priest, was one of the wealthiest and most feared men in all of Thebes.

"Where to next?" Amenhotep IV said to the aged Ptahmose, slipping back into his ceremonial Sed cloak. The priests now attempted to set the pharaoh's schedule for the busy festival day ahead.

"The temple of Wepwawet awaits, sire. We must apply holy ointment to the standard."

"I do not honor that god," Amenhotep proclaimed. "Wepwawet is nothing to me."

The priests shuddered at this heresy. Even Nefertiti was shocked, though her religious belief was much the same as her husband's. Egypt was a land of several gods, and all were to be worshipped according to law.

Before Nefertiti could say something diplomatic, Amenhotep grabbed her hand and yanked her down the smooth stone corridor toward the street. *"I know what I'm doing!"* he told her as the raucous crowd grew so loud, the pair could hear nothing else.

The royal couple entered the reviewing stand through the back and stood where they could observe the assembled masses without being seen themselves.

Nefertiti was awed at the sight of the crowd. "They are here for you," she told her husband. "They love you, as I do."

Rich and poor, scribe, surgeon, and farmer, had come from all over Egypt. They had cheered with delight when their pharaoh oversaw the morning's cattle census. An even larger group gasped in wonder as he donned the Sed cloak at noon. But that was six hours ago.

Now the crowd numbered in the tens of thousands. A combination of too much sun and too much ale had turned their enthusiasm into restlessness. Artisans, shopkeepers, even slaves were chanting as one, demanding to see their pharaoh make the dangerous chariot run.

How could he possibly fail—if he was divine?

Chapter 11

Thebes
1347 BC

NEFERTITI GLANCED AT HER HUSBAND, expecting to see him trembling in fear. Instead, Amenhotep wore a look of serenity. "When I am done with this, I will have put my mark on all of Egypt," he told her. "No longer will I allow those pompous buffoons in the temple—"

"You speak that way about the priests?" Nefertiti whispered. She had little respect for the priests but knew better than to talk like this. What was happening to her husband? Was he saying all this because he knew he was about to die?

"That's right. You heard me. No longer will they

have any say in how I rule my kingdom. Starting tomorrow, Amun, Re-Harakhty, and all their other pitiful gods will be banished."

"You speak heresy," Nefertiti said. She felt faint. Had Amenhotep gone mad? Was it his terror speaking now?

"We will worship Aten—and Aten alone." Aten was the sun god.

"Do the priests know? Any of them? Does Ptahmose know?"

Her husband's cunning smile answered her question.

"They will be furious!" she said. "They will come after you. *And me as well.*"

"That won't matter. Do you want to know why?"

Actually, she didn't. In his current state, Amenhotep IV was likely to say something utterly crazy. He didn't disappoint.

"I'm building a new city for us."

"I don't understand, Pharaoh," said Nefertiti. "What new city? Where would it be? Why haven't you told me before?"

"It will lie halfway between here and Memphis," he continued. "It will be the greatest city in the world. I will never leave there. Not even to wage war or collect tribute. Thebes and Memphis can return to the desert for all I care."

The crowd was loudly chanting the pharaoh's name, but Nefertiti wasn't ready to let him go. She clung to her husband and said nothing more. But then he pulled away and began walking up to the reviewing stand—without so much as a kiss or a good-bye.

"Oh!" he said, turning around to her. "I have saved the best for last. Tomorrow I will change my name to honor our god's greatness. No one will ever again confuse me with my father."

"What will I call you?" the queen asked, her mind reeling and her knees weak.

"Akhenaten."

And then, to deafening applause, the pharaoh strode to his chariot and began his ride to immortality.

Chapter 12

Thebes

1347 BC

AN EVEN GREATER ROAR echoed through Thebes as the pharaoh's horses picked up speed.

High atop the reviewing stand, Nefertiti watched... *Akhenaten*...and tried to appear calm.

Meanwhile, two deep-set eyes leered at her. They belonged to her husband's royal scribe, a powerfully built man in his late thirties named Aye.

The populace was mesmerized by the horse-faced pharaoh galloping his favorite chariot, but Aye could have cared less. He was tantalized by the nervous young queen—and then aroused when she slipped her index finger into her mouth to bite her painted nail—before

50

remembering that thousands might witness her insecurity.

The royal scribe licked his lips. He could have almost any woman in Egypt, but she was the one he wanted. Aye studied her graceful neck and the rest of her, down to the gentle sway of her hips. She was much smarter than the pharaoh, who was a freak undeserving of her, Aye thought. Having served under his father, Aye knew how a pharaoh should look and behave—and Amenhotep was no such man.

But if not Amenhotep, then who should reign? Aye wondered.

He answered his own question: *me.*

Nefertiti suddenly turned his way. She caught him staring but pretended not to notice. She never seemed to notice him.

Aye smiled and glanced down to the street. Miraculously, the pharaoh had survived the first leg of his journey and was now making the turn for home.

Just then a wheel flew off, bouncing wildly into the crowd and nearly beheading a spectator. Screams rent the air. Terrified onlookers fled, certain that the chariot would careen into them and kill dozens of innocents.

The pharaoh was thrown forward out of the basket onto the flank of the horse in front of him. He somehow managed to hold on to the reins but he dangled facedown over the side of the animal. The frightened team galloped faster and faster, dragging the chariot, hooves perilously close to the pharaoh's face.

Aye turned toward Nefertiti, whose hands now covered her mouth. Even as the future of Egypt hung on what happened in the next few seconds, Aye couldn't take his eyes off her. She was extraordinary in every way, truly a queen, possibly the most impressive person in all of Egypt.

Then the crowd exploded with a roar so loud that the ground beneath the reviewing stand shook.

Aye flicked his eyes back toward the street and saw that the pharaoh had somehow righted himself and pulled himself up onto the back of the horse. He now sat astride the white charger, fully in control as the team galloped on. Down came Nefertiti's hands. Away went the look of horror. She was a woman renewed, glowing with pride and love.

As the pharaoh halted the horses at the base of the reviewing stand, the crowd screamed in adulation. He looked up at Nefertiti, his eyes relieved and confident. He dismounted and walked slowly down the center of the boulevard, basking in the divine certainty that he was both ruler and god.

And then Nefertiti placed her lips to Aye's ear. He could smell her perfume and feel the heat of her skin. More than ever, he lusted for this beautiful woman.

"Starting tomorrow, Aye," she told him, "Egypt will be changed forever. Mark my words."

He had no idea what she was talking about. The only thing that mattered was the beating of his heart and the way his name had sounded in her mouth.

"And Aye?"

"Yes, my queen?"

"If I ever see you looking at me that way again, I will feed your heart to the crocodiles."

Chapter 13

Amarna
1345 BC

ONLY IN THE ANCIENT WORLD was such a thing possible—such a miracle in architecture. In just two years, the city of Amarna was complete. Aye had been in charge of the site, and now he sent word to the pharaoh. He figured he had three weeks, maybe four, until Akhenaten and his host of minions arrived.

But he had underestimated the earnestness of his king's desire to flee Thebes.

A week after his message was received, Aye was sipping ale on the terrace of the new royal palace. He was bored and lonely. His wife was still in Thebes. Even worse, so were his harem girls.

He gazed out at the Nile, marveling at the view. It truly was a gorgeous afternoon. The sky was a clear blue, and the heat tolerable if he stayed in the shade.

Then the royal vizier saw a sight so shocking that he nearly dropped his ceramic mug.

Cruising up the Nile was an armada of ships. Dozens. No, make that hundreds of vessels. Their great triangular sails were visible from miles away. Aye could see thousands of citizens from Thebes lining the decks, ready to start their new lives in Amarna.

And on the prow of the largest barge, to see first-hand all that he'd created, stood Akhenaten. The stunning Nefertiti and their three coquettish daughters were at his side.

Akhenaten raised the royal standard in triumph, but Aye was focusing on Nefertiti and those three girls.

No boys. Just girls.

"I'll kill him," Aye said in a flash of inspiration. Of course. It was the perfect solution.

Magnificent as she was, Nefertiti had not yet borne the pharaoh an heir. And with no male heir, there was no clear succession. If the pharaoh died—suddenly—there was no one to stop Aye from declaring himself pharaoh.

No one but Nefertiti, the queen bee.

"I'll deal with her when the time comes," Aye mumbled, already planning his crime. But he couldn't afford to make a mistake. To kill the pharaoh and go undetected would require a perfect murder. He would have to be patient, choosing just the right moment and the right means of execution.

Aye pursed his lips. If nothing else, he was patient. The plan had been revealed to him in an instant, every detail and twist, but it would take some time to execute.

"Some day *I* will be the pharaoh," he said boldly.

Chapter 14

Amarna

1892

THIS WAS AMAZING — *Amarna!*

Howard Carter carefully studied the lay of the land to make sure he had found just the right spot. What he wanted was a place with a view that was also close to the tombs. He had already examined the sand for drainage lines so that he wouldn't accidentally be swept away by a torrential downpour or the Nile when it overflowed its banks.

Now, at last, he settled on a spot. *This was it.*

Turning his head slowly in either direction to survey the horizon, he nodded to his small army of construction workers, who sprang into action — or at least moved as quickly as their somewhat relaxed approach to life and labor allowed.

Imagine—he was building a home here, a simple structure made of mud bricks like the ancient Egyptians used. For the first time in his life, Howard Carter was putting down roots, although shallow ones.

He would be laboring in Amarna, former home to Akhenaten and Nefertiti. The once grand, now ruined city was located at a broad bend in the Nile, on a low plateau fronted by a stunning array of cliffs. There was a shortage of housing in the newly rediscovered city, hence Carter's need to build his own. It would not be just any home, however, but a practical domicile in which ancient Egyptians would have been comfortable. He had begun by purchasing a thousand mud bricks for just ten pennies.

It was January, the peak of the dig season.

Carter had left Beni Hasan—and Perky Newberry—for Amarna, thanks once again to the patronage of Lord Amherst. He would work there under veteran Flinders Petrie, making elaborate drawings of discoveries large and small.

Immediately on Carter's arrival, Petrie had made it known that they would travel by foot at all times. Petrie, a frugal man, didn't feel a need to purchase donkeys when walking was just as quick and far less expensive.

Carter also learned that he would be "cooking" for

himself. *Cooking* was a euphemism for opening the tin cans that contained breakfast, lunch, and dinner on a Petrie dig site. Canned food was cheaper than purchasing local fare and hiring a cook.

Beyond that, canned food was more efficient. Flinders Petrie liked to work from eight in the morning until eight at night, each and every day. The less time spent on frivolities like cooking, the more time spent on excavation.

In addition, Carter received word that he was no longer just a sketch artist. Petrie had seen dozens of book-educated Englishmen come into the field, certain that their knowledge had prepared them to be excavators, and most had failed miserably.

Now, due to a shortage of excavators and an intuitive belief that the cocksure young Carter could be trained more easily than someone older and less ambitious, Petrie informed Carter that excavation was being added to his daily list of chores.

Surprisingly, the results thus far had been less than stellar. "Carter's interest is entirely in painting and natural history," Petrie had written in his journal on January 9, less than a week after Carter's arrival. "He is of no use to me as an excavator."

An early review—of the man who would make the most famous discovery ever in the Valley of the Kings.

Chapter 15

Amarna
1345 BC

THE FIERCE AND BELLICOSE General Horemheb could not believe what he was hearing from this silly, useless pharaoh.

"We will not be waging war on our neighbors," Akhenaten decreed, slouching in his throne.

The general should not have been cowed by the words of the pharaoh, but the intensity with which Akhenaten stared into his eyes was unsettling. Some men took power from privilege. Others took it from their position. And still others took it from physical prowess. The pharaoh pretended he possessed all three. This gave him a surety that Horemheb found disconcerting to say the least.

So while Horemheb longed to topple the pharaoh's misguided government with some great military take-over, he found himself listening to this most incredible statement delivered by a freakish weakling, and there was nothing he could do about it.

"But Pharaoh, if I may, we depend on war for many things: our wealth, our security, our status. This will mean the ruin of us. Your father—"

"I don't want to hear about my father. My father is in his tomb. His ways and his gods are things of the past. Just as dead as he is."

"But, sire, we are the most powerful nation in all directions. Certainly we must protect that."

Things have changed for the worse since the move to Amarna, Horemheb wanted to shout. *The country is going soft. The king never even leaves the palace. The great cities of Memphis and Thebes are in decline. We, as an Egyptian people, are in rapid decline.*

But he said none of these things. Instead, Horemheb listened to the pharaoh drone on in his stupid, idealistic way.

"And we will. We will worship Aten, who will protect our borders. But I see no need to wage war. What is so wrong with being a peaceful nation?"

"I believe in peace through strength, sire. We know this works from long experience."

"I would expect to hear nothing less from you, General. That is your job."

"And what is strength if it is not wielded? May I ask you that?"

The pharaoh smiled in a most condescending manner. "General, when was the last time you spent a day just dreaming?"

Horemheb's jaw nearly dropped off his head. "I beg your pardon?"

"You heard me. Do you ever write poetry? Do you ever lose yourself in thought? Have you ever completed a painting?"

"I am a warrior, sire. I am not trained to sit and think; I am trained to do."

"Then do *this*."

Akhenaten said nothing. Instead, he closed his eyes as if to meditate.

Horemheb waited until he could wait no longer. "Sire, what is it you would like me to do?"

"Relax. Take your mind off war. Egypt no longer needs conflict, for we are protected by the great sun god, who will provide for all our needs."

And lead us to ruin, Horemheb thought angrily.

"You are dismissed," said the pharaoh with a gentle wave of his hand. "Go write a poem."

Chapter 16

Amarna

1341 BC

"TUT. MY POOR TUT. What shall become of you?"

Nefertiti held her newborn son in her arms and feared for his life. Technically, the child was not her own, for he did not spring from her loins. But that idiot husband of hers with the wandering eye was the father, so the child might as well be the son of the queen.

The birth mother's name was Kiya, and the pharaoh had given the pretty young harlot the title Greatly Beloved Wife, which placed her above even Nefertiti in esteem.

Kiya was—had been—a Mitannian princess named Tadukhepa, sent to Egypt by her father, as a peace treaty between the two nations. For three long years Nefertiti had endured the woman's presence, watching her repeatedly take the queen's place in the pharaoh's bed. The man whom Nefertiti once loved had become a stranger to her, devoted to his beloved Aten and his child bride.

Why, the pharaoh had even begun telling people that he himself was Aten, that the pharaoh and the god were one and the same. It was Nefertiti who had the nerve to correct him, and for that he had cast her from his bed.

I am still the mother of his children, she reminded herself.

Yes, but all girls. This one, the son, will be the next pharaoh. I am no better than Tiye. When the pharaoh dies, the empire will fall to this child, this baby. And what will become of me?

What does it matter. There will be nothing left of the great Egyptian nation by the time my husband dies. That fool has seen to that.

The people of Egypt were starving and reverting to their nomadic ways, forsaking their farms and cities for a hardscrabble life on the move, all thanks to Akhen-aten's neglect or perhaps his insanity. The priests of Thebes wanted to kill him for usurping their gods with his own—and for asserting himself as a god. The royal vizier pretended to be a faithful servant, but once he got tired of Akhenaten's preening, he too would want to stab the pharaoh in the back.

And what of Horemheb? Surely the general went to sleep each night and dreamed only of a military takeover.

So what stopped them? Could it be that they actually believed the pharaoh was a god? What fools men are. Or what liars.

The baby started to cry. Poor Tut.

Nefertiti was about to whisper to the child, telling him that at that very moment his mother was being placed inside her tomb. She had died giving birth, and Tut would never feel the comfort of her arms or suckle her bosom. But the time for such talk was past.

"Be still, my son," Nefertiti said. "I am your mother now, and I will raise you to be the pharaoh your father should have been. You will be king. I promise you."

Chapter 17

Deir el-Bahri
1894

THE BLAZING SUN was beating down on Howard Carter's neck. It was Ramadan, the Muslim holy month, which meant that dig season was over, since the men fasted during the day. This made them too weak to dig in the hot sun.

Now Carter, working alone, alternately photographed and sketched the northwest chamber of a newly excavated temple near Luxor. He was nineteen years old.

It was Carter's second season excavating the structure dedicated to Hatshepsut, a female pharaoh nearly as famous as Nefertiti. It was a rocky location, situated at the base of a cliff, two miles from the Nile. Daytime temperatures often soared above 110 degrees Fahrenheit, and there was no shade.

Still, Carter worked dawn to dusk, in the fashion he had learned from Petrie, mainly because he so loved what he did. This was his life. There was nothing else for him.

His boss now was a Frenchman named Edouard Naville. The prolific excavator had long believed that a vast temple complex lay beneath the soil at Deir el-Bahri, and the results of several seasons' work were proving he might be correct.

Grand columns and towering walls now rose from the ground, unearthed after centuries of landslides and storms had covered them over.

Naville had been pleased with Carter's growing professionalism but was also concerned that the young Englishman was too slow when it came to sketching and photographing. The same methodical bent that Petrie had once encouraged was now seen as a serious flaw.

But this cloud had a silver lining. Naville had requested a second artist to help Carter. The man hired for the task was none other than Carter's thirty-year-old brother, Vernet.

The two had worked side by side through the early months of 1894, producing a series of dazzling sketches that were soon to be reproduced in book form.

Howard Carter had come a long way, actually. Not only had he learned to excavate, photograph, and supervise dig crews, but the young man was showing that his childhood sickliness was a thing of the past. When Naville closed the site for Ramadan, he asked the Carter brothers to continue working.

But the strapping Vernet fell prey to the heat and deprivation. He was forced to return to England, leaving his brother to finish Naville's job alone.

Carter had enjoyed the time with Vernet, but he never once contemplated returning home with his brother.

The life of an Egyptologist had its perils to be sure. It wasn't everyone's idea of the ideal job. But for Howard Carter, it was *paradise*.

And one day, he hoped to be a modern-day king— in the Valley of the Kings. He dreamed of making the greatest tomb discovery of them all, even though he had no idea what it might be.

Chapter 18

Deir el-Bahri
1899

THERE WAS NO SHADE to be had in the valley of Deir el-Bahri, not so much as a dancing speck. So as Carter set up his easel atop the ruins of an ancient and quite spectacular mortuary temple, the clock was ticking.

The rising March sun was just now lining the horizon. Within an hour, the heat of day would get uncomfortable, and beads of sweat would drench Carter's hatband.

Within two hours, his brushstrokes would dry almost as soon as he applied the watercolors.

And within three hours, the lead of his pencil would become too soft to sketch even a single line.

So he worked quickly, drawing the exterior of the temple, making sure that its massive proportions were in scale with the equally massive cliff rising like a great wall behind it.

The precision and symmetry of the sprawling complex, with three levels and sculpted columns, evoked images of an army of craftsmen, at the height of their talent, proudly building a structure that would last for all time.

What an idea. No wonder he could never leave this magical place.

Carter had acquired a reputation as a very good artist—indeed, his subjects ranged from the animals in the Cairo Zoo to intricate tomb interiors. But he had been in Egypt eight years now. It was impossible for him to paint a watercolor like the one on which he now labored without mentally filling in the history behind it.

A bead of sweat trickled down his face, but he was already lost in a reverie.

The temple before him had belonged to Queen Hatshepsut. It had taken fifteen years to build, but then the queen had been buried someplace else. The building looked more like a palace than a tomb and was peculiar for being so ostentatious. At the time of its construction, back in the fifteenth century BC, pharaohs were trying to conceal their burial places, not flaunt them for tomb robbers.

But just as this was no ordinary temple, Hatshepsut had been no ordinary pharaoh. After her husband (who was also her half brother) died, she had broken centuries of tradition and ruled as the first female pharaoh. Her reign had been prosperous, as were those of her children and her children's children

Carter knew that Hatshepsut had once been deeply in love, for she was a queen before she was a pharaoh. He knew also of her father, Tuthmosis I, the first pharaoh to be buried in what came to be known as the Valley of the Kings rather than in a pyramid.

The pyramids, so obvious and tempting, had been easy to plunder, which meant the pharaohs were deprived of their possessions during their journeys into the afterworld. Carving a tomb in a desolate valley seemed the best way to discourage thieves.

Sadly, the architect Ineni had been wrong about that.

So had Hatshepsut.

Despite the fact that the massive mortuary temple sprawled like a small city across the valley floor, no trace of Hatshepsut had yet been found.

Carter dabbed more paint on the paper—quickly. The sun was low on the horizon and directly in his eyes. He averted his gaze to reduce the risk of ophthalmia, bleeding of the eyes that came from looking too long at the sun. The disease was common among Egyptologists and could easily end a career.

A few hundred yards off, tourists and their Egyptian guides were dismounting mules and making their way to the temple.

Little did they know that one of the world's most promising Egyptologists was in their midst. Carter had worked his way up from being a poorly paid junior draftsman and was now learning the methods of the great excavators.

The key to becoming an excavator, Carter knew all too well, was luck. But after that came money, a great deal of money. He needed to find a wealthy benefactor to cover his costs. He had seen such patrons in Luxor, hanging out at the Winter Palace Hotel or enjoying the Nile nightlife aboard lavish yachts.

Carter didn't know how to mingle comfortably in that society—or any society, really—but it was time that he learned.

How hard could it be to fool a bunch of fools?

Chapter 19

Valley of the Kings
January 1900

"GENTLEMEN ARE INVITED to take off their coats," Carter advised the tour group as they approached the tomb. "It will get rather warm inside. Ladies, I'm afraid you'll have to settle for removing your hats."

His work ethic and passion for Egyptology had already lifted the ambitious twenty-five-year-old Carter from the obscurity of his early days to the relative power of his new position as chief inspector for the Antiquities Service in Upper Egypt.

Carter had beaten out Perky Newberry for the job, and now he oversaw all excavation in the region.

Many within the British Egyptology community

found this distasteful, even ridiculous. They objected to Carter's lack of book knowledge, his lack of a university degree, and, perhaps most of all, his lack of table manners. To them, Carter was not one of the world's foremost Egyptologists, just its most infamous and crude.

At a Christmas dinner in 1897, Newberry's brother had marveled at Carter's lack of social graces: "He doesn't hesitate to pick his last hollow tooth with a match stalk during dinner, bite bread that is so hard you can barely cut it with a chopper, and help himself to whiskey in an absentminded fashion, emptying half the bottle into his tumbler, then laugh and pour it back again."

Even Gaston Maspero, Carter's new boss, admitted that his charge was obstinate.

But Carter also had supporters and admirers, many of them female.

Lady Amherst still welcomed Carter to Didlington Hall whenever he returned to England. He was something of a hero to her family for his ongoing series of adventures in the Egyptian desert.

Carter was certainly someone to reckon with, even if he didn't know which fork to use for his salad. He was now museum curator for the entire Valley of the Kings. The area was an isolated jumble of hills, cliffs, and dry riverbed located three miles west of the Nile, just below the "horn," the highest point in the Theban hills.

Nobody knew exactly how many Egyptian rulers were interred beneath the sunbaked earth. And there was a good chance no one would ever know. Time and weather, crumbling rock, and blowing sand had completely changed the valley floor and enhanced its natural camouflage.

To actually stumble upon a tomb was to find the proverbial needle in a haystack, which is why any discovery was so precious and why everyone, from tourist to tomb raider, was eager to see inside each burial chamber.

Since Italian circus strongman-cum-Egyptologist Giovanni Belzoni had performed the first serious excavation of the area in 1815, the tombs of more than two dozen pharaohs had been found within its craggy, soaring walls. Belzoni had stopped excavating in the valley after thirteen years because he believed there was nothing left to find.

The discovery of tomb after tomb since then proved he'd been wrong.

In exchange for a "concession" — permission to dig in the valley — excavators agreed to split all treasure fifty-fifty with the Egyptian government. Sometimes the discovery process was as simple as clearing away a few scattered rocks. At other times finding a tomb required scraping away mountains of hard-packed sand and stone, clear down to the bedrock.

The allure was treasure first, history second.

Chapter 20

Valley of the Kings
January 1900

CARTER COULDN'T AFFORD to purchase a concession.

Nonetheless, just a few weeks into his new position, he was busily making the valley his own. In addition to setting up a donkey corral that could accommodate a hundred animals, he had begun installing heavy metal gates on all tomb entrances—to keep out the pesky robbers and squatters who prowled the valley at night.

He was also introducing electric lighting to make the tombs more inviting to the European tourists who visited the valley during the day.

And for reasons having nothing to do with his job

and everything to do with his own future success, Carter had begun to woo wealthy foreign tourists, hoping they might be convinced to fund a concession for him.

American businessman Theodore Davis was just such a tourist.

Davis was a small, hugely opinionated man with a dense white mustache spanning ear to ear. A regular visitor to Luxor (the site of ancient Thebes), he had begun to display an obsessive interest in Egyptology.

Now Carter stood with Davis and his group at the entrance to the tomb of Amenhotep II, a spectacular and yet dangerous place to be leading novices, especially rich, influential ones who might break a leg or suffer heatstroke.

The tomb had been carved into a high cliff, and they had all climbed a long, shaky ladder to the opening, with Carter leading the way. "It was a fine hot day," wrote Emma Andrews, Davis's traveling companion, who also took pains to point out that Carter was "pleasant, despite his dominant personality."

These tourists were hardly dressed for tomb exploration, the men wearing hard shoes and ties, and the women floppy hats and long dresses. Carter gave them each a candle and issued sharp instructions not to lag behind.

He led them down a narrow, low-ceilinged corridor, which descended steeply into the side of the cliff.

"Pay careful attention to each and every step, please," Carter advised as the earth suddenly disappeared: the tomb builders had excavated a well thirty feet deep and ten feet wide to dissuade — or trap and mangle — the uninvited.

Carter had laid boards across the chasm, and one by one the party made its way safely to the other side. In truth, he was playing up the danger a bit to pique the interest of these potential investors.

The tunnel plunged deeper into the earth, revealing an ancient stairwell that had given way and forced the group to scramble over a pile of loose stones. Paintings lined the walls here, ancient murals in subtle shades of maroon and yellow.

Carter was an impatient tour guide, despite his desire to woo a potential benefactor. Slower and weaker members of the group were tolerated but just barely.

At the site of another crumbled stairwell, the tourists had to pick their way, hand over hand, up the rocky pile, then squeeze through a narrow opening to continue the journey. By now most were sweating and breathing hard. The close air made some of them sick. More than one finger and forearm had been burned by dripping wax as the sightseers struggled to manage their candles.

Yet they gamely pressed on, following Carter, quite literally, into the bowels of the earth.

The corridor turned a corner, and suddenly the

group was inside a great rectangular chamber, and this room made the difficult trip worth every step.

The ceiling was painted with blue and yellow stars. And there, in the middle of the room, was a stone sarcophagus — with the mummy still inside.

"Notice the band of hieroglyphics around the top of the sarcophagus," said Carter in a hoarse whisper. "That is the mummy's curse, and that's the *only* thing that has protected it from being stolen."

As the group gaped in awe, wondering if their mere presence might somehow invoke the curse, Carter had to suppress a smile. What incredible idiots they were! The hieroglyphics said nothing of the sort. He was lying through his teeth, hoping that his fabrication might incite Davis to purchase a concession.

To Carter's delight, he did just that.

Chapter 21

Valley of the Kings
1901

HUNDREDS OF BATS FLEW LOW to the sand, fully sated after a night of foraging and eager to sleep. They skimmed over the Valley of the Kings, then banked hard to the left, finally whooshing down into the tomb where Howard Carter lay resting peacefully.

Echolocation guided them through the hieroglyph-covered hallways, then the bats burst as one into the main chamber and roosted on the ceiling, just feet above Carter's cot.

The adventurer barely stirred. Carter now had a home near the river, complete with an enclosed garden and a small menagerie of animals that included a horse named Sultan; a donkey, San Toy, who wandered freely through the house; and two gazelles.

But his home in Medinet Habu was miles from the valley and his work, so Carter often slept inside the tombs.

He had ceased worrying about the bats long ago and was slightly comforted by their presence. They were "strange spirits of the ancient dead," to his way of thinking.

The bats' arrival also meant sunrise, and sunrise meant another day full of the promise of discovery.

Suddenly, bare feet could be heard sprinting down the tomb's entry corridor. Carter recognized the anguished voice of a young Egyptian digger whose name he couldn't immediately remember. In part, this was because Carter wasn't a friendly man. He didn't socialize with staff or anyone else, except for the occasional female tourist.

"Inspector? Are you in there?" the young man yelled in Arabic. "*Sir? Sir?*"

"What is it?" Carter bolted upright and reached for his lightweight trousers.

"Come quickly, sir. There's been a break-in. Someone came during the night!"

Chapter 22

Valley of the Kings
1901

CARTER WAS STUNNED. He'd done his job so well, so painstakingly as inspector in chief that not a single tomb had been robbed in the Thebes area since he'd taken charge. Not one.

What had happened? Thieves in the night? Who? How?

Carter dressed in seconds and ran for the door. In the pale predawn light he picked his way across the rocks and scree of the wadi.

The path soon became wide and smooth and then led into a flight of steps that climbed steeply upward before dead-ending against a cliff face.

A doorway had been carved into the rock, marking the entrance. Carter had recently installed an iron gate across the opening to keep thieves out of KV 35, as the tomb of Amenhotep II was officially known.

But now that impenetrable barrier swung uselessly on its hinges. "How could this have happened?" muttered Carter. Then he called to the digger. "Bring men to guard the door. *I'm going inside! Hurry!*"

Back in Cairo, small fortunes were being made from tomb artifacts, with tourists and collectors quickly snapping up anything and everything grave robbers put on the market. Catching a gang of these soulless thieves red-handed would be quite a coup for Carter.

He lit a cigarette and paced until the reinforcements arrived. Amenhotep II was the grandfather of Amenhotep the Magnificent, and the great-grandfather of Akhenaten, whose queen was the alluring Nefertiti. Carter had *personally* removed the mummy of Amenhotep II from its coffin and laid it neatly inside a gold sarcophagus for the new tourist display.

The thought of some cretin actually touching the pharaoh, despoiling the remains, filled him with rage, and Carter had a temper that was widely feared in the valley.

He entered the tomb slowly, cautiously. As he did, silence washed over him. The first steps into a tomb were always like that—a reminder that he was leaving the world of the living and entering a place meant for only the dead. Sometimes he felt like he was trespassing and supposed that he was.

There were nine chambers in the tomb, each connected by a narrow hallway with a ceiling so low that Carter had to duck his head almost to his waist to pass through. He flicked on the light switch and waited for his eyes to adjust to the pale artificial glow.

Then he listened for the distant scurry of an intruder. But he heard just himself as he walked farther into the rocky tomb.

Stairs led down to a sharp left turn at what he liked to call the first-pillar room. Keeping one hand on the wall in case he slipped—and a sharp eye out for deadly cobras—Carter made his way down more steps and into the burial chamber.

The ceiling twinkled eerily with the handiwork of a long-dead artisan: hundreds of tiles representing a starry night. Straight ahead lay the mummified body of Amenhotep II, thrown on the floor like a rag doll. The burial chamber had been ransacked, everything stolen. What a terrible crime had been committed here.

And on Carter's watch.

Chapter 23

Valley of the Kings
1901

HIS HEART BEATING LOUDLY, angry as he could be but also heartbroken, Carter scoured the tomb for clues and telling details of the crime, sometimes crawling on his hands and knees. This sort of detective work was part of his job description. Thanks to his naturally dogged disposition, it came naturally to him, almost as if he'd been trained by Scotland Yard. And of course the tombs, with their dusty passageways and stale air, were like his second home.

Whoever was responsible for this crime had to be a professional. He'd known exactly what he was looking for and where to find it. By all appearances it was the work of an insider, but Carter's local diggers were a well disciplined bunch whom he trusted.

He immediately dismissed them as suspects—until he realized that the gate's lock had *not* been broken.

A key must have been used, and a key meant that his staff *was* somehow involved. Damn it!

Betrayal welled up in his throat like bile as he continued pacing through the chambers, appalled by the extent of the theft. All through the day and then into the night, Carter wandered the tomb, returning to the opening every now and then to smoke a cigarette in the fresh air before plunging back inside.

He never stopped racking his brain for some clue he might have overlooked—one that was most likely in plain sight.

He went to bed reluctantly and slept just long enough to realize that he couldn't sleep anymore.

By first light Carter was back at the tomb, vowing not to leave until he'd solved the heinous crime. He flicked on the light switch and again stepped inside.

Then he stopped.

In his investigation the previous day, Carter hadn't looked closely at the gate. He had *assumed* that the robber had a key. He suddenly remembered that the week before, someone had jimmied the gate open and sprung the lock. Nothing had been stolen at the time, and because the gate had shown no signs of significant damage, the matter had been forgotten.

Carter squatted down to inspect the lock. The previous day he had noticed a few scraps of lead paper and resin particles littering the ground and had thought nothing of it.

Now he rolled the resin between his fingers and gave it a sniff. He recognized the scent immediately—it came from the sont tree.

"What would this be doing here?" he said as he scrutinized the substance further. "The resin is the key somehow. But how?"

He studied the lock at eye level. Then he examined the resin.

Soon Carter realized that someone had shaped the resin into a small ball, one identical to the tongue of the padlock. "Ingenious," he said. "Simple, yet effective. This thief is clever. Almost as clever as I am."

Now he could imagine what had transpired. The earlier break-in wasn't a break-in at all but a *pretense* for snapping the lock and molding the resin to make the lock *look* like it hadn't been damaged. The robber then waited until the time was right and returned to the tomb. At that point, giving the lock a couple of good pulls would have been enough to cause the resin to give way.

Carter crept back into the tomb, feverish with anticipation, seeing the crime with new eyes.

His mind flashed back to a foiled robbery attempt some months earlier. A set of footprints had been found at the scene.

There was even a suspect, a man named Mohamed Abd el Rasoul, a local from a family known for generations of tomb robbing. El Rasoul was fond of studying excavations and then making "accidental" discoveries of his own, but the tombs were always looted by the time Carter and his crew were called to investigate. El Rasoul constantly walked the line of being suspicious and under suspicion, but no one had attempted to link him to those earlier footprints.

If Carter could just find another set, somewhere in Amenhotep's tomb, and then match them with el Rasoul, he would have his thief.

So Carter searched the tomb. Within minutes, he had found the footprints of a shoeless man.

Carter gauged the prints with his tape measure. They were the *exact* size of those found at the other robbery. "Down to the millimeter," he marveled. "I've got you, el Rasoul!"

Carter walked slowly back to the mouth of the tomb. He pulled out another cigarette and lit it, all the while staring out across the Valley of the Kings.

The sound of picks and shovels digging into the desert floor echoed across the valley, as yet another archaeologist searched for some long-lost tomb and the valuable spoils within.

Carter was rightly pleased with himself. How many other men could lay claim to the titles artist, excavator, *and* detective.

Chapter 24

Valley of the Kings
1902

FORTY-THREE.

As Howard Carter stood atop the Theban horn, looking straight down into the Valley of the Kings, that was the number on his mind.

It had rained the night before, a violent colossus of a storm that had literally formed rivers and caused landslides along the hills.

The upper layer of soil had been washed away, making it the perfect place for Carter to be strolling at that very moment. With his eyes fixed on the ground, and the number forty-three rattling around his head, he was scanning the freshly scrubbed earth for a telltale fissure or cleft that might yield a new tomb entrance.

Once again his heart was pounding. He was thinking how much he loved his job and that one day it would lead to great things. It had to. He had paid his dues.

Carter still felt an indescribable power in the Valley of the Kings and believed that the area had a life of its own. He found it alternately spiritual and playful, a mischievous wasteland that continually taunted Egyptologists who believed there was nothing left to discover. Time and again, great explorers had declared that they'd found all there was to find.

And then the valley would reveal another tomb or another cache of mummies, and the frantic spending and digging would resume.

Carter had carefully studied the detailed records of every Egyptologist since Napoleon and his men came through here at the turn of the nineteenth century. He had also studied the pharaohs' line of succession, comparing their names with the list of mummies that had already been found.

Simple cross-referencing told him that several pharaohs were still somewhere below him in the valley floor, just *waiting to be discovered.*

So now he gazed out over the valley, wondering about the mysterious forty-three.

Forty-three was not a person's name. In fact, Carter had no idea what it might be. Tomb discoveries were numbered sequentially, and in the previous three years an astounding ten new tombs had been located by Frenchman Victor Loret. But after finding KV 42 in 1900 and allowing Carter to help him do the major portion of the excavation, Loret had quit the valley.

KV 43 was still out there, waiting for someone to find it.

Carter suspected, sadly, that he would not be that man. The cost of hiring several hundred diggers for a season was more than five thousand pounds sterling. Add to that astonishing sum the cost of a yearly concession, lodgings, food, donkeys, shovels, picks, and wheelbarrows to move the excavated stone, and it was obvious that Egyptology was the calling of the rich. What chance did Carter, the son of a simple portrait artist, have of finding a great pharaoh's tomb? But still *he could dream.* And he was *here* rather than in dreary old England.

Carter stared out at the folds and tucks of the valley, as if merely by looking long enough he would spot some obscure sign of a tomb. Finally, he settled down onto the ground, sitting cross-legged on the only smooth patch of yellow dirt for a hundred yards in any direction. He opened the cover of his sketchbook.

Holding his pencil lightly to the page, then running it over the paper in quick bursts, he drew a simple outline of the valley floor and of the low flat mountains to the west. His challenge, as always, was to somehow capture the peace and grandeur that permeated that place. But for all Carter's genius as an artist, pencil lines on a piece of white paper could never fully convey the wonders of this magical spot.

There was great history here, if only he could find some of it himself, if only he could find KV 43.

Chapter 25

Valley of the Kings
February 1, 1903

CARTER BLINKED rapidly several times as he stumbled out into the pale morning light in this place that he loved. A loyal Egyptian worker, hoping to revive his boss, immediately handed him water and a cigarette.

As Carter took a greedy swallow, another local man slipped a long, double-breasted overcoat around Carter's shoulders. This might have given the young Englishman an air of casual elegance were it not for the fact that onlookers swore he looked like a ghost.

He was, in truth, thoroughly exhausted, having

spent most of the night sleeping outside on the hard ground.

At 4:00 a.m. he left a pair of men to stand guard, then went inside to prepare for the great unveiling—draping electric lights, placing beams over the deep wells, hanging rope ladders and handrails, and constructing wooden walkways so his eighteen guests wouldn't destroy fragile archaeological items.

Howard Carter had finally found his tomb.

Tuthmosis IV was the eighth monarch of Egypt's Eighteenth Dynasty. He reigned from 1401 to 1391 BC, and was the father of Amenhotep the Magnificent and the grandfather of Akhenaten. His body was sealed inside a stupendous tomb in the southeast corner of the Valley of the Kings. Elaborate pains had obviously been taken to hide the burial site, including a location several hundred yards away from any other dead pharaoh.

Tuthmosis IV had deliberately chosen the most desolate, distant spot possible. Not only did he wish to be buried for all eternity, but he also wanted to stay hidden.

Nevertheless, seventy-nine years after his death, tomb robbers found him.

On January 17, 1903, so did Howard Carter.

Tuthmosis IV was KV 43.

This was the first great find of Carter's career.

He'd had to wait two weeks for his patron, Theodore Davis, to return from a boat trip upriver to Aswan. Now Carter would lead yet another tour, only this time it would be to a tomb that he had discovered.

Davis had purchased an exclusive valley concession in 1902 and immediately hired Carter to lead the excavation. That first season had been inconclusive, with Carter discovering only the tomb of a minor noble and a box containing two leather loincloths.

For the 1903 season, Carter chose to excavate a small, forgotten valley within the Valley of the Kings. In days his men had uncovered a tomb entrance, complete with small vessels embedded in the rock, which the Egyptians believed held magical powers.

He led the large group into that opening now.

The path descended quickly. One heavyset functionary had comical difficulty wriggling through a particularly narrow passage into the deeper reaches of the tomb, and Carter had to pull him through. By now Carter was working mostly on adrenaline, proud of his discovery even as he delivered a clipped monologue about the tomb's contents: the war chariot, the sarcophagus, the mass of beautiful debris strewn about the burial chamber—no doubt by the tomb robbers.

The air was rank, and Carter would have to bring in fans and run lines of air from the outside as the excavation continued. But for now it was plenty good enough. As he escorted the satisfied group back up the steep passage to the main entrance, Carter's workday was done. He felt a little like a god himself.

Tea and a lunch awaited, served atop white tablecloths. The group, clearly awed by what they'd just seen, celebrated Carter and Davis as they dined.

Carter deflected the praise onto his egomaniacal boss, who was beginning to see himself not just as a benefactor but as an Egyptologist in his own right. There were plenty of accolades to go around, and everyone proclaimed what a successful dig season this was going to be.

"All praise goes to Mr. Davis!" said Howard Carter, believing not a word of it.

All praise goes to me, and perhaps to Tuthmosis IV, he thought.

Chapter 26

Valley of the Kings
February 12, 1904

CARTER COULD BARELY BREATHE, and poor Perky Newberry was about to pass out from the bad air, but their goal was within reach, and they soldiered onward into the most recently discovered burial chamber.

The subtext of this great moment was that Howard Carter had done it again. It was almost unbelievable, but just a few weeks after finding the tomb of Tuthmosis IV, he'd unearthed another tomb on the same side of the valley. Inside was a mummy in a coffin.

The dead man's identity was unknown thus far, but Carter had made an amazing find. Not long before, he had come across evidence of Hatshepsut's burial place.

The female pharaoh's temple on the other side of the mountain was perfectly aligned with this latest tomb. To Carter's way of thinking, it was possible, even likely, that a tunnel connected them.

"I do not hope for an untouched tomb," he had written Edouard Naville, alluding to every Egyptologist's prayer of finding a virgin burial chamber. "Rainwater will be a great enemy, but hope for the best."

Carter was certainly right about the rainwater. The storms that wiped the hillsides clean of debris had sent chunks of rock and sand into tomb openings where they had hardened like cement. Since mid-October his workmen had swung pickaxes in the tomb corridors, clearing out the compacted earth.

Bits of pottery and other funerary debris had been found in the dirt, keeping alive Carter's hopes that the elusive mummy of Hatshepsut might be buried here. Finding it could be the highlight of his career and make Howard Carter famous around the world.

Finally, after four months, the workers had reached the burial chamber. Perky Newberry and Carter pulled down the mud-and-stone blocking that formed the chamber's doorway. Then both men entered.

A wave of dank, noxious air washed over them as the hole widened. Several steps inside, Newberry couldn't take it anymore.

He pleaded with Carter to follow, then staggered back toward the light. But Carter pushed onward.

How could he not? He had worked thirteen long, hard years for this day, this discovery.

The heat and dank air conspired against him. Every stitch of his clothing was drenched in sweat, and he gasped for each breath.

The tomb, as he had predicted, was not untouched. Inside was an *empty* sarcophagus, a canopic jar, and broken vases bearing the names of Hatshepsut and her father.

They were items of historical interest, nothing more.

And *more* is what he wanted.

Howard Carter would no longer be satisfied with simply locating tombs. Now he wanted tombs of significance, untouched throughout history, and he especially wanted the great treasures buried with every pharaoh.

Carter "emerged from the tomb," wrote a friend of Theodore Davis's, "a horrid object, dripping and wet, with a black dust over his face and hands—he was very sick, too, and had to lie down for some time."

But the very next day, Carter was back at work, searching for that elusive virgin tomb that would make him a household name.

Maybe it would be Hatshepsut.

Or perhaps another pharaoh of even greater importance.

The treasure hunt continued, and, in truth, it became Howard Carter's whole life.

Chapter 27

Amarna

1335 BC

NEFERTITI WEPT as she had never wept before.

"Aye!" she finally yelled. "Bring me Aye. I need him right this minute. Now!"

The royal scribe came running into the pharaoh's bedroom. Nefertiti was slumped at the foot of the bed, her supple frame hidden in an elaborate robe. The pharaoh lay on his back, unclothed, covered only by a scrap of bedsheet Nefertiti had laid across his lower body.

"He's dead," Nefertiti said before Aye could utter a word.

Their eyes locked, and in that brief exchange,

in the fire of Nefertiti's eyes, the power in the royal palace shifted inexorably in the new widow's favor. She was no longer the wife of the pharaoh but ruler of all of Egypt. She was divine. And Aye was still just the scribe—that is, if she allowed him to live.

Aye cleared his throat. "What happened?"

"What do you think happened, Scribe? Isn't it obvious to you? I could barely get him off me."

Indeed, the pharaoh had gotten heavy in his late thirties, and the lithe Nefertiti weighed less than half of his considerable mass. Perhaps even that was being charitable to the late pharaoh. Aye had a clear mental picture of the queen's bronzed biceps straining to shove her dead mate off her after his final collapse.

"I'll see to his burial, Majesty," he said. "I will do everything."

"And send out the messengers," Nefertiti commanded, her lower lip quivering. "Send them to Thebes and to Memphis. Announce to one and all that the great pharaoh is dead."

"Majesty, do you think that wise? I mean, until we know who will succeed Akhenaten?"

The royal scribe looked at her insolently. To be sure, Aye was a powerful man in the kingdom, and he balked at taking orders from this woman or any woman.

Nefertiti glared at him. "Have you forgotten that my husband fathered a child out of wedlock?" Her voice dripped with sarcasm. She had also given Akhenaten an heir since arriving in Amarna, but the child had died.

"When the time comes, and he has grown into a man, I will place my husband's son on the throne, but for now *I am the pharaoh,* Aye. Make no mistake about that." She paused and looked at Akhenaten once more. "Now, leave me with my husband. Go. Do your duties."

Aye lowered his eyes and spun on his heels, then charged from the sun-filled room. He would do as he was told — for now anyway.

Chapter 28

Amarna
1335 BC

NEFERTITI GAZED down at her husband. Then she sat on the bed beside him, gently running her hand across his shaved head. She traced a lone finger down to his chest. Then she stroked his face, memorizing every detail.

These would be their last moments together, and she wanted to remember him as the powerful man he had once been, not the weak and whimsical pharaoh he had become. Nefertiti shuddered to think what would soon happen to this body she had known so well.

She placed her index finger atop the bridge of his nose. The royal mummifiers would start here, slipping a long wire up the nostrils into that marvelous and eccentric brain. They would spin the wire until the brain's gelatinous tissue broke down and revealed itself as gray snot running out of the nose.

They would then turn the body over, positioning the head at the edge of an alabaster table to let the brain pour into a bucket, glazed with gold.

Nefertiti now placed her hand low on her husband's groin, anticipating the spot where they would slice him open, shove a hand up inside, and yank out the internal organs.

Who would do this task? Would it be some vile little man with a filthy beard and dirt under his fingernails? Or a professor, a stately academic chosen to mummify the king because he was more knowledgeable about the ways of the afterworld?

She smiled as she placed her hand atop his sternum, the spot where she had laid her head so many times and felt the beating of his heart. At least they would leave his heart intact. Like her people, she believed the heart was the source of all knowledge and wisdom. Akhenaten would need its greatness to cast the spells that would reanimate his corpse.

Seventy days, she thought. That was how long it took to finalize the mummification process.

Seventy days to dry out the body in the desert heat so that it didn't decompose before reaching the afterworld.

Seventy days until they placed her husband in his tomb six and a half miles from where she now sat.

Let the other pharaohs entomb themselves in the Valley of the Kings—Akhenaten had chosen a spot just outside his beloved Amarna, a glorious valley all his own, bathed in sunlight so that he might delight in the wondrous majesty of Aten forevermore.

"I will join you there someday," said Nefertiti, leaning down and kissing the lips that had traveled up and down every inch of her body.

She gazed down at him one last time and then left the room. Her husband was dead. Their oldest son had predeceased him, and of his remaining children, just one was a boy.

It was now her duty to rule alongside the child until he became a man. She beckoned for her lady-in-waiting, a tall girl whose beauty compared favorably with her own.

"Yes, Queen?"

"Bring me Tutankhamen."

Part Two

Chapter 29

Palm Beach, Florida
Present Day

ONE OF THE MOST FASCINATING PIECES discovered in the tomb of King Tut was an armless mannequin. Presumably, it was used for draping his clothes. Tut's face was painted on the mannequin, and it sported a crown. The face is a boy's, and it seems gentle and kind and knowing.

As I do on many mornings, I was walking Donald Trump's golf paradise in West Palm, my favorite course anywhere. But my mind was on Tut. What an incredible mystery this was turning out to be. I was becoming nearly as obsessed as Howard Carter must have been.

With all due respect, Dr. Cross and Lindsay Boxer, I'll

return to your crime scenes after I've finished with Tut. I'm still gathering evidence.

This was a completely different writing process for me, primarily because of all the research involved. I had been fortunate to hook up with Marty Dugard, a talented and generous writer and researcher who had already traveled to London, then to the Valley of the Kings to help me make the story as authentic as possible and, more important, to gather details that might solve the murder mystery.

The story had so much potential — much more than most detective novels. After all it was about kings and queens, buried treasure, an explorer who reminded me of a pissed-off Indiana Jones, and the murder of a *teenage* boy and probably his sweetheart.

As soon as I got back to the office, I found a thick folder assembled by my indefatigable assistant, Mary Jordan. The evidence that this *was* a murder story was starting to mount.

A March 8, 2005, press release had announced the results of a full body CT scan of Tut's mummy by Egyptian authorities. This was the study that prompted Zahi Hawass — secretary general of the Supreme Council of Antiquities — to announce that Tut died from an infection resulting from a broken leg. The particular infection, in his opinion, was probably caused by gangrene.

It seemed like a slam dunk for the secretary general, until I read a little further: "The broken left femur shows no signs of calcification or hematoma," both of which would have begun developing immediately after the accident.

In fact, part of the expert team reviewing the results of the CT scan refused to agree that the broken leg was the cause of death. They believed the leg was accidentally broken *after* the tomb was discovered, when someone had tried to move the body. But in a 2007 interview, Hawass again conceded that Tut had died from a broken leg.

The next bit of evidence I discovered was even more curious: X-rays had previously shown a thickening of the skull consistent with a calcified membrane, which can occur when a blood clot forms around an area of high trauma. This is known as a chronic subdural hematoma. However, the CT scan showed no evidence of a blow to the head. Maybe the Egyptian investigating committee was spending too much time trying to justify the broken-leg theory and not enough on the wound at the base of Tut's skull.

The earlier X-rays were the product of R. G. Harrison, a British anatomist who had done extensive work on Tut back in the 1960s and 1970s.

Not only had Harrison x-rayed the skeleton, but he had taken the rather extreme measure of *separating the skull* from the other bones and x-raying it individually. Based on his findings, Harrison suspected foul play.

This made sense to me. A subdural hematoma

111

could develop if somebody whacked you very hard on the skull and you survived the blow, only to die some weeks later. In the meantime, the bruise from the blow would become a blood clot, and that blood clot—the chronic subdural hematoma—would calcify.

All of which made me wonder why anyone would say that Tut had died from a leg fracture.

A contrarian position seemed more likely, and that got me excited. Based on the results of the 2005 report, combined with the 1969 and 1978 X-rays, it appeared that Tut's leg had not been broken during his lifetime, and that he had suffered a blunt force trauma to the back of the skull.

So if Tut had been murdered, possibly clubbed to death, who did it?

Chapter 30

Valley of the Kings
1907

OH, how the mighty had fallen!

Howard Carter stood outside the Winter Palace Hotel with a clutch of watercolors under one arm. His jacket was threadbare, with unsightly patches at the sleeves. The shoes on his feet weren't much better, the leather unpolished and worn.

He set up his easel near the great marble steps leading up to the hotel lobby, praying that some fool tourist might take a shine to one of his paintings. The sale would net him much-needed money for whiskey and cigarettes, and perhaps even a civilized lunch inside the hotel.

Howard Carter may have become a street bum, but he still had standards.

His problems had begun when he was transferred away from the valley by the Antiquities Service. His new posting, near Cairo, meant that Davis had to find a new executive Egyptologist. Even worse, the ancient tombs at Saqqara proved to be an administrative nightmare for Carter.

When he had allowed his Egyptian tomb guards—quite justifiably—to use force against a drunken mob of French tourists, it became an international incident. After nine months of increasing shame and disgrace, Carter had been forced to resign.

Truth be told, he desperately wanted to get back to the valley. He still hoped to find Hatshepsut's mummy—and maybe even the ever-elusive virgin tomb.

That tomb, if recent events in the valley were any indication, might belong to a long-forgotten pharaoh named Tutankhamen. King Tut had somehow slipped through the cracks of history—or been purposefully edited from it.

His name was *nowhere* to be found among the many shrines and temples where the succession of pharaohs had been chiseled in stone. In 1837, British Egyptologist Sir John Gardner Wilkinson had noticed the name on a statue. But other than that single mention, Tutankhamen was virtually unknown.

Ironically, it was the American Theodore Davis—the man Carter had originally persuaded to finance a valley concession—who had stumbled upon interesting new evidence about Tutankhamen.

Chapter 31

Valley of the Kings
1907

THE INCREDIBLE STORY, as Carter heard it, began with Theodore Davis and his new chief executive Egyptologist, Edward Ayrton, taking a midday break from the stifling heat.

The valley, as always, was crowded with European tourists eager to see the ancient tombs. Davis was the sort of man who enjoyed being fawned over, but now he ignored the gawking stares that seemed to follow him everywhere.

Davis could hear the distant bray of donkeys from the corral. That chorus mingled with the constant clang of workmen striking their tools into the hard-packed red-yellow soil. Those were the sounds of the valley during dig season, and after four seasons searching for tombs, they were sounds Davis knew quite well.

Davis and Ayrton "owned" the Valley of the Kings, in a manner of speaking. Davis still held exclusive rights to dig there, and with Carter exiled, the Petrie-trained Ayrton was now Davis's top man.

The season had been solid so far, with the tomb of the pharaoh Siptah discovered on December 18 — the day after Ayrton's twenty-fifth birthday. Now, the January sun having driven them to find a sliver of shade in the valley's southwest corner, the two men took a moment to plan their next excavation.

Ayrton smoked quietly as the eccentric Davis stared off into space — or so it appeared.

"My attention was attracted to a large rock tilted to one side," Davis later recalled, "and for some mysterious reason I felt interested in it."

The two men trekked back out into the sunlight. The rail-thin Ayrton had just been hired by Davis a few months earlier but was already used to the man's impulsive behavior.

If Davis wanted to have a look at the rock, then they would have a look at the rock.

Ayrton appraised the boulder from several angles. Then, noticing something peculiar, he dropped to his knees and began moving the loose soil away from the base.

There, buried for ages, was a spectacular find!

"Being carefully examined and dug about with my assistant, Mr. Ayrton, with his hands, the beautiful blue cup was found," Davis later wrote. The cup was of a glazed material known as faience and, with the exception of a few nicks, was intact.

The ancient Egyptians had used such cups at funerals. This one was stamped with the name of a pharaoh—*Tutankhamen.*

The cup seemed to imply that this Tutankhamen—*whoever he was*—had been buried nearby in the Valley of the Kings.

Davis had made his fortune as a lawyer and practiced Egyptology as an avocation, so his techniques were far from typical. He was a short man with a giant white mustache and an evil temper that had led several talented Egyptologists to quit after working with him. There had also been several complaints about the way he ransacked tombs rather than cataloging the contents for history.

But however people felt about Theodore Davis or his methods, there was no denying his Valley of the Kings monopoly. And until it was totally exhausted, he would not give up his concession.

With the "beautiful blue cup" clutched firmly in the palm of his hand, Davis added the name of this mysterious new pharaoh to his list of tombs to be found. And Davis was sure he would be the one to do it.

Howard Carter, making his living selling watercolors to tourists, could do nothing about this new development. He merely stored the information away.

Tutankhamen was out there somewhere just waiting to be found by somebody.

Chapter 32

Amarna

1335 BC

THE MORNING SUN, so benevolent and omniscient, blessed Nefertiti as she awaited Tut's arrival in her private quarters. Akhenaten had been dead for only a few hours. She had already selected a group of "mourners," women who would openly grieve at her husband's funeral, beating their exposed breasts and tearing out their hair.

The time had come for the queen and her boy to have a grown-up talk about his future and, indeed, the future of all of Egypt

Nefertiti loved the six-year-old Tutankhamen: his trusting brown eyes, his passion for board games, even his endless questions about why the royal family never traveled to cities like Thebes and Memphis. In fact, Nefertiti adored everything about Tut except for one niggling detail: he wasn't her son by birth.

As a very bright and practical woman of the times, Nefertiti understood that a pharaoh might have needs that could not be fulfilled by just one woman. But as a passionate queen and a woman unaccustomed to being trifled with, it had infuriated her when Akhenaten had married and impregnated Kiya. The great god Aten had been just and wise when he had taken Kiya's life as she gave birth to Tut. And Nefertiti made sure that there would never again be a second wife around the royal court.

She had tended to her husband's every fantasy, and when she couldn't, Nefertiti directed his affections toward the harem girls, for it was common knowledge that no pharaoh, not even one as outlandish as Akhenaten, would marry a common whore.

So it was that Nefertiti began to raise Tutankhamen as her own.

The boy never knew his real mother, and though he had been told of her life and tragic death, he was still too young to fully comprehend being conceived in the womb of one woman and reared by the loving hands of another.

"Did you want to see me, Mother?" He was so innocent—and yet so full of life. Nefertiti was overcome with warmth as she gazed upon the boy. She did love him, deeply, but not everyone in the court did. For some, he was already a hated rival.

"Yes, Tut. Come. Sit next to me. Sit close to your mother."

Tut walked across the tile floor in his bare feet and plopped onto the divan next to Nefertiti.

"I heard about the pharaoh," he said softly. "I'm sorry."

She placed a hand underneath his chin and lifted it until his eyes met hers. "Your father hadn't been feeling well for a long time," she told him.

"How did he die?" Tut asked next. Always the questions with him.

She could never tell him the truth, but a lie didn't feel right either. "He died in a burst of happiness. His heart was so filled with joy that it exploded."

There. Not so bad.

"Tut, there's something else we need to talk about. I need you to pay attention to what I have to tell you now."

"Yes, Mother?"

"You are just a boy and have not yet been trained in the ways of the pharaoh. But you must know that this is your destiny."

The boy stopped her. "I don't understand."

"You will be pharaoh one day, Tut."

"I don't want to be a pharaoh. I don't! Why can't you be pharaoh, Mother?"

"It is not considered best for a woman to rule Egypt, Tut. But because I am of royal blood, I will find a way to rule for as long as it takes you to learn to be a great pharaoh."

"How long will that be, Mother?"

"A dozen years, maybe less. Because you're so bright, Tut. There is no hurry. The important thing is that you learn to be wise and strong and full of compassion for the people of Egypt, as your father was. He was a good man, always a good man."

"Smenkare would have made a good pharaoh," said Tut. "And he was your son. This day must make you sad."

The boy was smart, which was probably why she loved him as she did.

"Smenkare is dead, Tut." She neglected to add that she had never loved her own son as much as she loved Tut. She had tried, but there was no light in Smenkare's eyes, and she felt no connection between them. Someone like that should never have ruled Egypt, and it was almost fitting that the job would now go to this precocious boy at her side.

"No, Tut. It must be you."

Tut simply nodded. "So what do I do next? Help me, Mother."

"See how we're sitting here? You and me, right next to each other?"

"Yes. Of course I do."

"This is how we will rule Egypt at first. Side by side, the two of us. For now I will make the decisions, because you are too young. But as you become a man, you will fill a bigger space and have the knowledge to make good decisions."

"Then I will rule as pharaoh?"

"Yes, Tut. And I know that you will do great things. You will be a pharaoh people always remember."

Chapter 33

Amarna
1334 BC

THAT WAS THE PLAN for the boy who would be king, though it didn't turn out that way. Not even close. Once again death would intrude—perhaps even murder.

"You live in a house full of women," the military instructor informed Tut. "To be pharaoh, you must become a man. Someday, you will be as big and strong as I. Once you are through with your training, no man will stand in your way."

Studying the instructor's bulging biceps and massive chest, Tut had a hard time believing that could ever be true, but he listened closely to every word.

They stood in a great green field on the west side of

the Nile. It was February, and the mild sun kissed the earth.

Tut was a skinny child whose slightly cleft palate gave him a mild lisp but who otherwise bore the flawless beauty of his mother. His arms were thin, and his sandal-clad feet supported legs that weren't much bigger around. At the time of his death, Tut would be approximately five foot six, and his build would still be slight.

"Are you ready, sire?" asked the instructor.

Tut tried to speak, but in his nervousness only a sigh escaped his lips.

The instructor concealed a smile. "Let's talk about the types of bows we will be using in our archery practice, then."

The list was too long and too dazzling for Tut to remember right away—though the instructor made it very clear that the pharaoh would be proficient in each of them, along with shield and mace, sword fighting, spear throwing, chariot riding, horseback riding, hand-to-hand combat, daggers, throw sticks, boomerangs, clubs, and battle-axes. For today's lesson—there was a double-composite angular bow, composite angular "bow of honor," bow staves, and short self bows. That was *all* he had to master.

The bows were made of birch that was then wrapped in sinew and bark for durability. Gold leaf and ivory decorations adorned their curved shafts. The instructor's great bow was taller than Tut, while Tut's bow was only big enough to reach just above his knee when he stood it on the ground.

The instructor placed the bow in Tut's little hands: "Now listen to me. You will want these with you in the afterworld. On the day you are buried, all your bows will be buried with you. So learn to use them well, Highness. The rules of combat you are about to learn will stand you in good stead . . . forever."

Tut notched an arrow in the bow and pulled back the string. His shot hit the target cleanly on the first try, though it wasn't far from the boy.

"Very good, sire. *You are a natural*."

Chapter 34

Amarna
1335 BC

"YOU'RE LATE. I won't tolerate this, Tutankhamen. There's no excuse for such conduct."

Tut raced into the royal classroom at the prince's school with mud from the Nile still coating the soles of his feet, his favorite hunting bow in hand. He had been out in the reeds again, shooting ducks, and realized too late that it was time for class.

He had no chance to clean up, and now, pharaoh-in-training or not, he would face the instructor's wrath.

"Instructor, I—"

"Quiet. Not a word from you. Sit down and practice your hieroglyphics."

The teacher was a thin, dyspeptic young man who didn't walk about the room so much as he flitted like a nervous bird. Tut liked to mimic him for the amusement of his sister, but now she was too busy giggling at Tut's misfortune for him to attempt a joke.

The standard punishment for tardiness was to write the twenty-five characters of the hieroglyphic alphabet on a piece of papyrus one hundred times. The task often took two hours, which the instructor knew was absolute torture for Tut.

He was eight now, and his latest passion was chariot lessons. Two hours spent writing meant two less hours spent at the reins, speeding across the open desert.

Much as his father would have hated it, Tut longed for the day when he would lead the warriors of Egypt into battle. He pictured himself in a chariot, two mighty steeds galloping before him, an army of thousands responding to his every command. But this was no daydream—it would actually come to be—and sooner rather than later.

"Well done, Pharaoh," whispered his sister, Ankhesenpaaten. She was a few years older than him, but mature in the way of deeply practical children. And she was a beautiful girl, even better-looking than Tut.

"Someday," the teacher announced, "when you reign over Egypt as the one true pharaoh, you can have me killed for my insolence, but until then this is my classroom and you will do as you are told— and that includes arriving on time. *Am I understood, Tutankhamen?*"

A furious, red-faced Tut nodded his head and placed a fresh reed in his mouth, making sure not to make eye contact with his sister, who now snickered at his misfortune. Tut chewed the end of the reed, feeling the fibers break apart until they formed a loose and supple paintbrush.

Then he dipped his new writing implement into a bowl of water and touched it to a block of solid ink. He began to draw on a piece of papyrus, his hand effortlessly forming the falcons, owls, feet, and myriad other images that made up the hieroglyphic alphabet.

But soon the afternoon heat and the quiet of the classroom had his mind wandering. He loved the outdoors, and to be stuck inside on such a beautiful day wounded his spirit.

Tut longed to be swimming in the Nile, ever mindful of the crocodiles that lurked there. Or maybe taking Ankhesenpaaten for a chariot ride—he adored her. Or perhaps simply standing on a mountaintop, gazing out at the purplish rocks of a distant butte, reveling in the fantastic notion that all of this land, as far as the eye could see, would one day be his.

This was not merely a boy's daydream either—it was for real.

Chapter 35

Amarna
1335 BC

AS HE DREW HIS CHARACTERS, Tut kept an eye on his strict instructor, the bane of his youth. The last thing he needed was another unjust punishment on top of the others he'd accrued. Nefertiti had been very clear in her warnings about Tut's studies. If he failed a subject or even fell behind, he would lose the right to go out beyond the palace walls. Tut could think of no more horrendous penalty.

Then, to Tut's amazement and joy, the same warm afternoon sunlight that had sent his mind wandering, now cast a spell over the instructor. Tut watched eagerly as the man rested in his chair and his eyelids began to close.

The instructor's head then lolled back and his mouth opened slightly, until, ever so softly, he began to snore.

Ankhesenpaaten put one hand over her mouth to keep from giggling. Tut gently placed his brush on an ivory palette and tapped her on the shoulder while jerking a thumb toward the door.

"No," Ankhesenpaaten mouthed. "We can't do that, Tut. We *mustn't*."

Tut insisted, standing quietly and taking hold of her arm. With a quick glance at the instructor, whose soft snore was deepening into something louder, she stood too.

Together, the boy and girl royal tiptoed toward the door and the freedom of the river world. To be safe, Tut grabbed his hunting bow on the way out.

Suddenly, Aye's hulking torso blocked their path. "Where do you think you're going?" the royal scribe boomed, making Ankhesenpaaten jump in fear.

The instructor jerked awake and leaped to his feet.

Aye gripped Tut and Ankhesenpaaten tightly by the arms and dragged them back in the room, digging his fingernails into Tut's bicep. "Let go of me," Tut cried, but Aye only squeezed harder. "I will be pharaoh one day, and you will be gone from the palace. I promise it, Scribe. You too, Teacher!"

Then Tut wrenched his arm free and ran, and he didn't stop running until he stood on the banks of the Nile. What was even better was that Ankhesenpaaten had run with him — every step of the way.

Chapter 36

Amarna
1334 BC

"WHAT DO YOU THINK they'll do to us if they ever catch us?" asked a smiling Tut, crouching down below the reeds so they wouldn't be seen by Aye or their other nemesis, the teacher.

Ankhesenpaaten was usually the practical one. Her impulsive decision to escape along with Tut had perhaps been the greatest surprise he had known since the day their father died.

But it was a nice sort of surprise, the kind that made him feel less alone in the world. It felt really good to have a comrade in arms—a friend—if only to share the inevitable punishment that would follow this outrageous adventure.

Tut looked into his sister's eyes and smiled. Technically, she was his half sister, thanks to his father's consort with the ill-fated Kiya, and though she and Tut were the fruit of the same father, it more often felt like they were best friends than brother and sister.

She was like him, and she wasn't. It was hard to explain. Except that he loved her dearly. He so dearly loved his Ankhe.

"They're not going to beat us," Tut announced, answering his own question.

"Why do you say *'they'*?" she asked. "It's Mother who will determine our punishment."

"That's not exactly the way it works," Tut said patiently. "Aye and the instructor are men. They think they have power over Mother."

As part of the process of learning to become pharaoh, Nefertiti had taken great pains to include Tut in important meetings with her advisers. Even a boy could see that Aye coveted the great power that Nefertiti possessed. The royal vizier often cast angry glares at Tut, as if the boy had somehow offended him by just being there.

Aye frightened Tut, and as he remained in the reeds thinking about him, he gently rubbed the marks Aye's thick nails had left on his upper arm.

"You need to watch out for Aye," Tut told his sister. "I don't trust him. Neither should you. I think he wants to marry Mother and become pharaoh."

Ankhesenpaaten smiled at this.

"He can't do that, Tut. You're the pharaoh."

"Not if he marries the queen. Marriage into royal blood would allow Aye to take the throne."

Tut paused to let that sink in, tilting his head to watch a duck extend its wings and lift them slightly upward as it glided in for a landing.

"I don't like that," Ankhesenpaaten said softly, "and I don't like Aye. Not a bit. He's angry, and he's rude to Mother."

"We also need to watch out for Meri-Re, the high priest," warned Tut

"Why him?"

"He's afraid that when I become pharaoh I will no longer worship Aten."

"He would lose all his power and wealth if that happened."

"Right. You're a smart girl. Almost too smart somehow."

"And General Horemheb is a sneaky one. Keep an eye on him also."

"I will be wary of them all," said Tut. Then he did something he really hadn't expected to do. He leaned in close and kissed Ankhe. And perhaps even more surprising, she didn't protest.

Then, confident that they had avoided capture, the two children rose from their hiding place and sprinted toward the river, laughing. They were less afraid of the crocodiles lurking there than of the powerful men crawling about the palace.

Chapter 37

Thebes
1908

HOWARD CARTER had been summoned.

His old friend and Antiquities Service boss, Gaston Maspero, wanted to meet and discuss Carter's "future." In the four years since Carter had left his post, there hadn't been much talk like that—more a hand-to-mouth existence that barely kept Carter's dreams alive and often made him look foolish for having them.

So Gaston Maspero's request for a meeting was more than welcome. It could be a lifesaver.

The distance from the Winter Palace Hotel to the Valley of the Kings was roughly five miles. If one stood on the great marble steps leading up to the hotel's main lobby, it was possible to gaze across the Nile toward the distant cliffs that formed the backside of the valley. When there was no wind and the desert dust was not clouding the air, those cliffs seemed almost close enough to touch.

That's the way Howard Carter felt every day of his exile. A man less passionate about Egyptology would never have debased himself the way Carter had, standing out on the streets to hawk his wares to tourists, no different from the hordes of carriage drivers, ferryboat captains, and beggars who lined the dirt road at the river's edge.

Like them, he existed on the most meager of handouts. His serviceable watercolors would probably have been completely overlooked and ignored were he Egyptian rather than European.

To say that Howard Carter's life had fallen into disarray would be an understatement. He'd become a shadowy version of himself: at once haughty and penniless.

To supplement his modest living as a watercolorist, he also sold antiquities on the black market, thus sinking to the level of the men he'd once prosecuted for tomb robbery.

Carter dressed well enough, even though his clothes were worn, and still had a taste for fine food and expensive hotels, but he'd become dependent on wealthy patrons to make his way. Adding insult to injury, his most beloved patrons of all, Lord and Lady Amherst, had fallen on difficult times. They'd been forced to sell Didlington Hall in 1907, and Lord Amherst was in poor health. At the age of thirty-four, Howard Carter had become little more than a self-educated sycophant.

Enter, thanks to Maspero, the inimitable Lord Carnarvon.

George Edward Stanhope Molyneux Herbert, better known as the Fifth Earl of Carnarvon—or, more simply, *His Lordship*—was a pale, thin man with a hound's face pitted by smallpox. He smoked incessantly, despite damaged lungs; raced cars; owned horses; and otherwise reveled in living the life of a wealthy, self-absorbed bon vivant. Even the 1901 car crash that had almost killed him didn't stop Carnarvon from spending his money recklessly and living a life of entitled leisure that no one deserved—at least not in Carter's opinion.

His Lordship had first come to Egypt in December 1905, thinking that the warm weather and dry air might help him recuperate. That visit and subsequent other "tours" whet his appetite for all things Egyptian.

In winter he maintained a luxurious and spacious suite at the Winter Palace Hotel. Little by little, Carnarvon was transformed from a man consumed by the here and now into a man consumed by the past—*the ancient past.*

Chapter 38

Thebes
1908

NOW, LIKE MANY WEALTHY MEN who'd become smitten by Egypt and treasure hunting, Lord Carnarvon wanted to fund his own excavation.

The successes of Carnarvon and Theodore Davis were well known, and Carnarvon could easily see Davis's yacht *Bedouin* moored across the street from his hotel. British acquaintances Robert Mond and the Marquis of Northampton also had minor concessions, and Carnarvon began to believe he would enjoy digging up an important bit of history. He thought it should be *great fun* indeed.

Unfortunately, his first season's results weren't

promising. Or much fun. Arthur Weigall—who now held Carter's former job as chief inspector for Upper Egypt—had dismissed Carnarvon for the rank amateur that he was. He assigned Carnarvon to a rubbish heap known as Sheikh abd el-Qurna, with predictably dismal results.

The sole find during that first six-week season was a *mummified cat* contained inside a wooden cat coffin.

Carnarvon, while disappointed, actually treasured the discovery. It was his first, after all. Egyptology was now officially in his blood.

The only problem, it seemed, was Carnarvon. Rather than hire an experienced professional, he led the digs himself. Each day he would sit inside a screened box that kept away flies, and smoke cigarette after cigarette, as his men, and *not* a top-notch crew, worked in the heat and dust.

What Carnarvon needed—he was told repeatedly—was a seasoned professional to guide his digs.

And Howard Carter needed a wealthy patron with a concession to get him back in the game.

Between seasons, Carnarvon wrote Weigall from England, asking for "a learned man, as I have not time to learn up all the requisite data."

The common thread in all of this was Maspero, who had arranged Carnarvon's concession in the first place.

So it was that Carter was summoned to the Winter

Palace to stand before Carnarvon and Maspero to discuss the possibility of once again leading a full-scale excavation. His clothes were nearing the point of no return, and his ever-present portfolio was tucked under his arm, as if he had been called to sketch the moment, which, he believed, was a depressing possibility.

Did Carter want back into the game? he was asked.

The disgraced Egyptologist, thrilled that fate was giving him a second chance, hastily answered yes.

He even managed to keep his famous arrogance and temper in check — for the first meeting anyway.

Chapter 39

Amarna

1333 BC

"WHAT'S WRONG, MOTHER?" asked Tut.

The handsome little boy stood beside Nefertiti in a garden surrounded by fig trees and date palms and a rich green carpet of grass. His mother sat in the shade of a small palmetto. Her beautiful face was a tightly clenched mask. They both knew that she was dying, and yet she pretended that nothing of the sort was true.

To be eight and on the verge of losing his mother, so soon after losing his father, was something that no child could be prepared for.

But Tut was no ordinary child—he had royal blood—he was divine.

So he joined his mother on the small settee. He watched as she slowly leaned back and tried to relax then flinched in pain as her skin came in contact with the hard chair.

"I'm dying, Tut, and I need to ask you to do something that you might think odd."

"Don't say that, Mother. You're *not* dying."

"I am. Either I am being poisoned—or there is a sickness inside my body that Aten does not wish to remove. I have ordered my servants to hasten their preparations of my burial chamber, because there isn't much time for me."

Nefertiti closed her eyes as pain shot through her body. Tut placed his hand on top of hers, but did so gently, so as not to hurt her.

This small act of kindness and compassion made Nefertiti smile. "You will be a great pharaoh. I am sure of it."

"Thank you, Mother."

He paused, reluctant to say what was on his mind.

"What is it?" Nefertiti asked.

"Do you promise not to be angry?"

She let a moment pass as she weighed her answer. "I promise. Now ask your question. You must always speak your mind, Tut."

"Did Aye do this to you? I see the way he looks

144

at you. It's hard to tell whether he loves you or hates you."

"I think it's a little of both. But no, I do not fear Aye—though you should. You are just a boy and need to be protected from powerful, unscrupulous men who might want to see you harmed."

"Do you think he wants to be pharaoh?"

"Yes, Tut, I do. And he is not the only man with a dream of ruling Egypt."

"But he is a commoner."

"So are you, Tut. Remember, your natural mother was of common birth. You are only half royal. Your sister is the only child in this palace who is full-blooded royalty. This is why I have asked you to come see me."

"What do you mean? What are you saying, Mother?"

"Ankhesenpaaten cannot reign as pharaoh because she is a woman. But for you to rule as pharaoh, and to produce an heir who ensures the succession of our royal blood, you must blend your blood with that of a woman who is fully royal. Do you understand?"

"But Ankhesenpaaten is the only such person."

"That's right, Tut." Nefertiti flinched once again from the pain. "Ankhe is the only one."

"So you're saying that..."

His voice trailed off in confusion, so Nefertiti finished the sentence for him.

"You must marry your sister."

145

Chapter 40

Luxor

1909

HOWARD CARTER was once again in the world that he loved more than anything else. A little older perhaps, a few belt holes thinner, but he was definitely back in the game.

As the sun rose over the glorious Nile, he gazed out across a site at a small army of workers, just as he had so many times before. True, he was digging in what many called the "unfashionable district" of the Theban necropolis, where, at best, he could hope to find the tombs of nobles and wealthy businessmen instead of pharaohs. But after years of living hand to mouth, Carter didn't mind at all.

It was good to have a job. So Carter lit a cigarette and gave the order for his men to start digging.

Lord Carnarvon stood at his side, dressed smartly in a suit and skimmer.

Their relationship would clearly be different than the ones Carter had enjoyed with Lord Amherst and even Theodore Davis. The old days of Carter being stubborn to make a point were over. He was a hired man now and would not be treated as a member of the family.

But he didn't much care. He had plans in his head, plans to bring professionalism and accountability to Carnarvon's ragtag style of digging. Wealthy patrons were hard to come by. With Carter's expertise and Carnarvon's money, there was a chance they might actually find something important.

And someday, if this all worked out, they would move into the Valley of the Kings and do some real digging, for *real treasure.*

Chapter 41

Thebes
1330 BC

THERE HAD BEEN no public ceremony and no special words from the high priests to mark the moment of their marriage union.

Ankhesenpaaten had simply moved her belongings to Tut's side of the palace, where their father had once laid his head.

That had been three years ago. They had slept in separate rooms since then but had also become closer friends. Now, on the day they had put Nefertiti in her tomb, Tut was officially the pharaoh.

Ankhesenpaaten fumbled with her gauzy, white gown as she and Tut prepared to share a bed for the first time. He wasn't yet a teenager, like his sister and bride, who was a few years older, but Tut had begun to physically develop into a man, and this wasn't lost on his wife.

It was time they produced an heir—or at least, given their ages, began practicing.

Tut untied the cumbersome, false pharaoh beard from around his head and laid it on a bedside table. Nefertiti had coached them both, in individual discussions, and Tut thought he had a good understanding of how it all worked. But he had never visited a harem, as the royal scribe Aye seemed to do each afternoon after lunch, and what was about to transpire was unnatural and awkward to him.

Ankhesenpaaten turned her back discreetly as she slipped her dress off her shoulders. Tut watched the fabric drop down past her narrow hips and land silently on the floor.

Ankhesenpaaten covered her budding breasts with one hand as she turned to pull back the bedcovers, then slid between the warm cotton sheets. He could smell the perfumed oils she used on her body and hair.

"Now you, *Pharaoh*."

Tut felt butterflies in his stomach and was unnerved at the thought of shedding his clothes right there with Ankhe in the room, especially since his own longings were on full display.

"Did you ever feast as much as today?" he asked

somewhat randomly, referring to the whirlwind of revelry surrounding Nefertiti's funeral. All the priests of Aten had feted her. Aye had been there too, and Tut had noticed that the royal vizier drank quite heavily while huddling in the corner with Tut's generals.

"I don't think I've ever seen that much food in my life," Ankhesenpaaten agreed.

"I wish Mother could have been there."

"Now you can make your claim to the throne. No one can deny you."

"Yes," Tut said softly, feeling for the first time the crushing weight of being the pharaoh of all Egypt. It pressed down on him like a block of limestone.

"We are alone, Tut," Ankhesenpaaten whispered, realizing a different sort of burden. "Just the two of us in this difficult and complicated world. Not a parent to guide us. No brothers or sisters. Just us."

"It's scary when you say it like that."

"Yes. But Tut, let's promise that we will always look out for each other and protect each other from those who would do us harm."

"I promise, Ankhesenpaaten. I will never let anyone harm you."

"I promise too."

The bedroom was still then, uncomfortably so. The warm desert air flowed in through the open window, and Tut could smell the faint and wonderfully familiar musk of the Nile.

Ankhesenpaaten took a deep breath, and then she pulled back the sheets, unafraid to show herself to her husband.

In their many years together, Tut had never seen his half sister naked, and now he gasped at the realization that she was exceptionally shapely and beautiful.

"Take off your kilt, Tut," she said.

The pharaoh did as he was told. And he was beautiful too.

Chapter 42

Thebes

1326 BC

THE NIGHTS OF PASSION were but a bittersweet memory to Ankhesenpaaten now. Still the young queen had never been more excited — or frightened.

"*I'm late,*" she whispered, rolling over in bed and propping her chin on Tut's chest. She could feel her breasts pressing against his ribs, as she reached down to touch between his legs.

"How often have I heard that?" Tut replied, doing his best to sound pharaoh-like, instead of utterly smitten.

"Tut," Ankhesenpaaten whispered, mounting him.

"I am three months late. We are going to have a baby. I'm certain of it. So tonight, let's celebrate."

Tut gazed up at her and supported her body by clasping her breasts. She leaned forward and began rocking slowly, all the while caressing his face with her hands.

"Think of a name," she said softly, closing her eyes as pleasure coursed through her body.

"Nefertiti," he said.

"What if it's a boy?"

"Nefertiti." Tut laughed.

"What about Tuthmosis? Or Amenhotep? Those are royal names."

Ankhesenpaaten moaned then; names no longer seemed important to her.

She was usually very quiet in bed, but on that morning she was sure she woke all of Thebes as she climaxed. The sensation seemed to go on and on, a wave of pleasure that rolled through her once-barren body just as surely as the Nile flowed through Egypt's desert sands.

She looked down at Tut and watched his shoulders tense as ecstasy contorted his beautiful face. Then he let out a most unpharaoh-like cry.

"We are going to have a baby," repeated Ankhesenpaaten.

Chapter 43

Thebes
1326 BC

THAT HAD BEEN five months ago.

Now, perched atop a royal birthing stool, Ankhesen-paaten clenched her abdominal muscles and pushed one last time—at least she prayed this was the last time. As Tut stood by her side, clasping Ankhe's hand, their child finally joined them, delivered into the waiting hands of the royal physician.

It was stillborn.

The poor baby was obviously deformed, with one shoulder much higher than the other and a spine curved sideways, and just as obviously dead.

"Summon the royal magician," the doctor said

emphatically, speaking to a courtesan standing just behind Ankhesenpaaten.

The royal magician would be charged with healing whatever illness had caused the queen to miscarry, burning hot coals on the floor between her legs as she remained on the low stool, allowing the smoke to enter her womb and clean out all impurities.

"Is it a boy or a girl?" Ankhesenpaaten asked in a weak voice. She felt like crying but held back the tears. She had always been a strong girl.

"I do not think it matters, Queen," said the doctor.

"Boy or girl?" barked Tut in a voice that indicated he would not brook such insolence.

The physician sat up straight, remembering his place. "A girl, Majesty."

Ankhesenpaaten held out her arms. The umbilical cord connecting mother and daughter was still intact, and now the queen pulled her dead child to her bosom and sobbed in anguish.

Ankhesenpaaten ran a finger over the baby's head, touching the small nose and stroking the soft black tufts of hair. The child's eyes were closed, and she kissed each one.

All too soon, she knew, the royal embalmer would mummify this newborn and place it into the royal tomb to await the death of her parents.

"We will get to know one another in the afterlife," Ankhesenpaaten whispered. "I love you, my darling Nefertiti."

Chapter 44

Egyptian Desert
1324 BC

IT WAS HIS TIME NOW, but was he ready—quite possibly *to die*? Tut stood alone in his tent, his stomach a knot of nerves and fear. Adrenaline raced through his body as he anxiously clenched and unclenched his fists, then bounced lightly on his toes a half dozen times. He was all of eighteen years old, and he was going to war.

Outside, he could hear swords clanking and horses whinnying as his great army assembled on the morning of battle. *His* army. *Egypt's* army.

Tut whispered a silent prayer to Amun. He strapped on his leather chest armor, slid a sword into the scabbard at his waist, then stepped out into the harsh desert sunlight to join his soldiers.

Unlike many of these men, whose wives followed the army, Tut had traveled alone. Sadness over the loss of their child had changed things between Tut and Ankhesenpaaten. Even though she had become pregnant again, things weren't the same. She was moodier, more grown-up.

Unlike his father, who stayed home with Nefertiti every day of his life, Tut began traveling. He hunted deer with Aye, whom he continued to distrust. And he fell under the spell of General Horemheb, particularly on the subject of warfare. To be a real man, Tut decided he needed to do battle. He needed to be here with the army.

Now he had a chance to fight for the first time. He would test his mettle today, and perhaps he would die.

The great Egyptian army was encamped near the Canaanite city of Megiddo, a desert fortress surrounded by towering walls of mud and limestone. There was a good chance the Canaanites would refuse to come out and fight, preferring to endure an Egyptian siege than to be slaughtered in full view of their women and children.

Tut prayed that this would not be so. He ached for his first taste of battle.

The gleaming sword weighed heavily against his hip as he inspected of his chariot team. Like soldiers before him, Tut vowed to be strong and to show no fear, but he worried that he might turn and flee.

"You have a talent for drawing, Pharaoh. Your images of the gods are so powerful that I feel the urge to bow down at the sight of them," said Horemheb, who had stepped up to Tut's side. It was a snake-like compliment about Tut's passion for art, a not-too-subtle insinuation that the boy was timid like his father.

"Are you saying I should have stayed in Thebes, General?" Tut was unafraid to ask hard questions, even of men decades his senior.

Now he wiped the sweat from his brow. He surveyed his men, infantry, archers, and charioteers assembling in long orderly columns. A simple sweep of the eyes brought into view an arsenal the likes of which few had seen before: powerful bows, maces, highly sharpened axes, spears, and daggers glistening in the sun.

Having so much power at his disposal excited Tut in a way that he never could have imagined. No, he was *not* his father's son. He was a warrior!

Chapter 45

Egyptian Desert
1324 BC

"I WAS PAYING you a compliment, Pharaoh," said the crafty Horemheb.

"Then I accept your compliment. Tell me, General, what is our strategy today?"

The general's large but powerful chest and belly were bronzed from the sun, and he squinted as he studied Megiddo's distant fortifications. "May I speak bluntly, sir?"

"Of course you may. You know me well enough by now. I need to know the truth—always. Speak your mind."

"I have conquered this miserable town before. It

is a den of whores and thieves who don't understand anything except brutal domination. If they come out to fight, we will first launch arrows and then send chariots to scatter their army. Our fighting men will wade in and slaughter them like the weak little piglets that they are. The desert sands will be engorged with their blood, which will flow from their bodies like water over a raging cataract."

Horemheb grinned maliciously. Instead of groveling, he was now testing Tut for signs of squeamishness.

"When that moment comes, General, I will personally gut a Canaanite. I will use his innards to grease the axles of my chariot."

"As you should," said Horemheb, who seemed to approve of the pharaoh's words.

Tut stared at Megiddo again and then turned to Horemheb. "And if they do not come out, what then?"

"Then there will be a siege. We will poison their wells and starve them. It might take months, but we will enter the city. I guarantee it. You haven't lived until you've plundered a city like this one. The women cannot refuse you. And the men know to bring the youngest and most beautiful. You, of course, will have your pick."

Horemheb paused, his sense of timing exquisite. "That is, if you desire a grown woman. They can be tempestuous, Pharaoh. Particularly when reluctantly submitting to a victor."

Tut resisted the urge to draw his sword and hack off Horemheb's arm to put him in his place. The general would be able to do nothing in his defense.

"My wife is woman enough for me. You may have my share of tempestuous whores."

Suddenly, Horemheb's eyes caught sight of something.

"What is it, General?"

"Permission to sound the call to order?"

"But what is it? What do you see? Tell me."

Horemheb pointed a gnarled finger. "The gates to the city. Look for yourself. They are opening! The Canaanites are coming out to fight."

Chapter 46

Egyptian Desert

1324 BC

"HOLD!" YELLED HOREMHEB, the low timbre of his powerful voice cutting through the dry desert air. The highly trained Egyptian forces halted abruptly. Tut stopped too. Then he stared in utter amazement at the scene unfolding before him.

A mile distant, the Canaanite army poured forth from behind the city walls.

The infantry marched three columns abreast, numbering perhaps five-thousand men. The all-important archers were assembled on the wings, ready to fire on any Egyptian flanking movement.

Up in the very front, mirror images of Horemheb

and Tut and the rest of Egypt's commanders, the Canaanite charioteers charged forward. There were two men in each chariot, a driver and an archer, which allowed arrows to be fired while racing into battle.

The Canaanites came fast, as if intending to take immediate control of the field.

Their hulking shoulders and the great, dark beards that covered their chests made them look bigger and stronger than the Egyptians.

To his shame, Tut's throat instantly closed in terror. He threw up in his mouth. As he studied the Canaanites, he realized that their march had not faltered, nor had their pace slackened. They seemed to grow more terrifying as they closed to within five-hundred yards.

But their horses! Tut could see that they were ill-trained and struggling to turn away from the fight.

Even the animals have the good sense to fear the coming battle, he thought. These were not the horses of victorious warriors, but horses that knew what it was like to turn and flee.

The realization galvanized Tut, but the chaos in his stomach intensified. He bent over and vomited in his chariot, quickly wiping his mouth and standing up straight so that his men would not think their pharaoh weak.

But there was no hiding anything from Horemheb. "I have done it many times myself, Pharaoh," he said, his voice laced with sarcasm.

No, now would not be a good time to cut off Horemheb's arm. Later, perhaps. After the victory was assured.

"It will not happen again," Tut barked, steel in his voice.

His schooling had included courses in tactics and warfare. Now, with Horemheb's taunt ringing in his ears, Tut took command of the battlefield. He removed the composite bow from his shoulders. Made of cherry wood and leather, its gleaming ivory decorations looked too beautiful for the battlefield, even as the copper-headed arrows in his quiver shone with lethal intent.

"Give the order for battle formations!" he told Horemheb.

The general glared at Tut but said nothing at first. He was not used to being ordered about, especially by a boy. "As you wish, my king," he finally replied.

Then Horemheb turned and faced the assembled army. "Battle formations!"

The Egyptian column spread out, until they formed a wide but narrow line, shoulder to shoulder, twenty men deep, facing down the men of Canaan.

The well-trained charioteers remained in front. The archers scurried to the right and left flanks.

Horemheb, and the entire army, awaited Tut's next command.

Conventional wisdom said that a wide-open

battlefield like this desert plain favored the defender, so in this case it was best to wait for the Canaanites to make the first move.

But Tut knew that such tactics did not always work. As his adrenaline surged, flooding him with a new fearlessness, his instincts told him that this day the Egyptians must attack first.

"I do not wish to give them a chance to flee behind the city walls," Tut stated evenly.

"As I said before, we will wait them out," insisted the general.

Tut licked his lips. Holding tight to the reins of his chariot, he stepped from the chassis and turned to face his troops.

Their bodies glistened with sweat, and they looked tired from the two-week march from Thebes, but there was no mistaking their professionalism. They were reliant warriors, hungry for battle and the rewards of victory. They had trained and drilled for the sweet primal satisfaction of fighting man to man against a sworn enemy of Egypt. And then—plunder.

Tut's heart raced. He had never been so proud to be an Egyptian.

The troops watched him expectantly, awaiting the next command. "General Horemheb, command the archers to open fire."

Chapter 47

Egyptian Desert
1324 BC

NOW EVEN HOREMHEB had caught the fever, and when his words rang out across the desert, they were delivered with the same excitement as Tut's.

"Archers, take aim."

The Canaanites could see the Egyptian archers draw arrows from their quivers and then pull back their bowstrings. A distant horn commanded the Canaanites to battle, and they flew at the Egyptians, daring their attackers to hold their lines.

Simultaneously, the Canaanite archers took aim.

Now Tut chose an arrow from his quiver, ready to fire the first shot of war. He launched it into the sky in a powerful arc, right on target. Only then did he call out to his men.

"Fire!" Tut commanded. His voice was thin and reedy, still that of a boy on the cusp of manhood. But there was fury in his tone, and a fearlessness that buoyed the Egyptian lines.

Tut's archers sent forth a volley that blackened the sky before descending into the Canaanite infantry and charioteers. Hundreds of them fell, screaming to the heavens, writhing in agony.

Tut watched in dismay as the Egyptian infantry refused to attack, preferring to hold their lines.

It was Horemheb who told him why.

"They're waiting for you, Pharaoh."

Tut swallowed hard. How long had he been taking chariot lessons? Six years? Seven? He believed he could ride as well as any man, but he couldn't be sure. "Be with me, Mother," he whispered. Then the young pharaoh stepped back into his chariot.

"Sound the call, General."

Horemheb signaled to the herald. The battle horn blared.

Meanwhile, the Canaanites continued to sprint forward, shouting and waving their long swords, hoping to terrify the Egyptians, and especially the young pharaoh.

Tut slipped his bow back over his shoulders. He pulled his sword from its scabbard. The time had come to christen it with the enemy's blood. He slapped his reins down hard on his team's flanks and raced straight toward the Canaanites.

As one, the Egyptian army roared forward behind him. High above them, another volley of arrows arced, then fell into the Canaanites' battle lines.

Horemheb and the other Egyptian charioteers galloped up beside Tut. Within seconds they were trampling the bodies of Canaanite warriors who writhed in pain. Tut could hear the whoosh of swords meant for him.

Holding the reins in one hand, Tut swung out with his sword. He was stunned to see the blade sever a man's neck. Tut had killed him, his first victim.

The Canaanites retreated, dropping their shields and sometimes even their swords, running for their lives.

But Tut could see that the great wooden city gates were shut tight. They could not escape.

The women of Canaan had chosen to doom their husbands and sons rather than submit to the Egyptians. It was left to Tut's men to finish the slaughter. Canaanite bodies soon littered the desert, most butchered beyond recognition. Many of the dead were twisted into impossible positions. Some seemed to have died with an arm or leg reared up toward the sky.

Tut had finally tasted battle and become a man — and a true king.

Chapter 48

Thebes
1912

THE BOOK THAT DOCUMENTED EVERYTHING, every large and small success by Carter, was known as *Five Years' Exploration at Thebes: A Record of Work Done 1907–1911*. Despite the lack of a valley concession, the partnership between Carter and Carnarvon had certainly been prolific.

Carter had refined his excavation techniques, bringing greater precision and professionalism to the task. He introduced photography as a means of documenting discoveries and continued to sketch elaborate drawings. With local work crews sometimes numbering close to three hundred, he and Carnarvon discovered tombs of nobles and other high-ranking functionaries.

But as well-received as *Five Years' Exploration* proved to be, raising eyebrows in London and Cairo for the depth of the Carter/Carnarvon discoveries, the American Theodore Davis continued to overshadow them, and that galled Howard Carter.

Now a story about Davis making the rounds suggested that Davis had not just found a new tomb in the valley but the *last* tomb.

Theodore Davis believed he had found the elusive Tut.

Chapter 49

Thebes

1912

IT ALL BEGAN when Davis and Edward Ayrton discovered a hidden doorway made of mud bricks and stamped with the image of a jackal watching over nine captives. This seal for the necropolis guard signified that a mummy was inside.

Next to that was stamped another symbol, this one representing Tutankhamen.

They immediately kicked down the door and tore away the bricks with their bare hands, then entered a narrow hall.

A sloping corridor led to the burial chamber. Rocks littered the floor. A piece of wood decorated with gold leaf showed the image of Queen Tiye, known to be the mother of the "heretic king" Akhenaten.

What an amazing four days it had been. On January 3, Davis's workers excavated an ancient trash heap. Inside they found eight large sealed pots bearing Tutankhamen's name. As it turned out, the jars were filled with embalming supplies and leftovers from a long-ago feast, as well as floral collars stitched with berries and flowers.

Very likely, this feast took place after Tut's burial. The flowers were a sort that bloomed between March and April, offering a clue as to when this mysterious pharaoh had died.

Now this.

At the end of a hallway was the main chamber. It was heavily damaged by water, but the seals of Tutankhamen could be seen everywhere on the walls.

A casket lay on the floor.

Once it had rested atop a wooden platform, but time had rotted that away, and the coffin had toppled over. The lid had popped open, and when Davis looked inside, he was delighted to see a mummy staring back at him.

Portions of the bandaging were unwrapped. Davis could see hair and teeth and the remnants of a nose.

He plucked a hair, then wiggled a tooth, trying to determine the mummy's condition. Not surprisingly, it gave way in his hands.

Davis was dismayed but only for an instant. Not even waiting for Ayrton's help, he lifted the mummy into his arms and carried it out into the sunshine as if it were a small child.

He stood there, dazzled, as tourists stared at him in utter shock and amazement.

A doctor happened to be walking by on the broad dirt path. Davis knew the man and beckoned to him. The doctor performed an inspection of the mummy — and determined that it was a woman.

Davis made a judgment: based on the evidence, he was holding in his arms the remains of Queen Tiye. He was now *convinced* that the tomb was that of Tutankhamen. All he had to do was dig deeper, and he was certain he would find the pharaoh himself.

Standing in the center of the Valley of the Kings, cradling a thirty-three-hundred-year-old woman, Theodore Davis was triumphant and flushed with acumen and success.

He was also dead wrong about everything.

Chapter 50

Luxor
1912

CARTER AND CARNARVON weren't the only Egyptologists to publish a book that year.

Carter leafed through the pages of Theodore Davis's *The Tombs of Harmhabi and Touatankhamanou*, and he was more convinced than ever that the elusive tomb of Tut was still out there somewhere in the valley.

Carter was "quite sure there were areas, covered by the dumps of previous excavators, which had not properly been examined." Looking forward to the day when Davis would abandon his concession, and he and Carnarvon might return to the valley, Carter added:

"I will state that we had definite hopes of finding one particular king, and that king was Tut.Ankh.Amen."

Carter lit a cigarette and reread the descriptions of the tomb in which Davis purported to have found Tut. In his opinion, the gold-flaked and alabaster objects present inside that tomb were of too low a quality for a pharaoh's burial chamber. Davis was a fool not to see as much himself.

More likely they had been placed there years later, when the tomb was reopened. Owing to the growing connection between Amarna and the tomb, it seemed plausible that Queen Tiye had been relocated from Amarna to the valley at some point after her death.

No, Tut hadn't been found. But other discoveries in the valley—jars of embalming fluid, the faience cup, remnants of a final meal bearing inscriptions showing it had been part of Tut's burial feast, seals bearing his symbol stamped on tomb doorways—clearly showed that he had existed.

"To explain the reasons for this belief of ours, we must turn to the published pages of Mr. Davis's excavations," Carter went on to write. "Davis claimed that he had found the burial place of Tut.Ankh.Amen. The theory was quite untenable...We had thus three distinct pieces of evidence: the faience cup found beneath the rock, the gold foil from the small pit tomb, and this important cache of funerary material. Which seemed definitely to connect Tut.Ankh.Amen with this particular part of the valley."

Now all Carter needed was an opportunity to find it. "With all this evidence before us, we were thoroughly convinced in our own minds that the tomb of Tut.Ankh.Amen was still to be found, and that it ought to be situated not far from the center of the valley."

But he needed Davis to abandon his concession.

Two years later, the American did just that.

Chapter 51

Valley of the Kings
February 8, 1915

LORD CARNARVON SNATCHED UP Theodore Davis's concession without hesitation. Just like that, after eight years of waiting, Carter was back in the valley. He finally began scouring the area for his long-hoped-for virgin tomb on February 8, 1915.

When Davis had walked away from his concession, saying that the valley was "exhausted," few members of the Egyptology community disagreed. "We remembered, however, that a hundred years earlier Belzoni had made a similar claim and refused to be convinced. We had made a thorough excavation of the site and remained convinced that there were areas, covered by the dumps of previous excavators, which had never been properly examined," wrote Carter.

Carter clung to the belief that Davis's evidence was incredibly slipshod and that he'd made assumptions about the discovered mummy's identity that couldn't be verified. "Clearly enough, we saw that very heavy work lay before us and that many thousands of tons of surface debris would have to be removed before we could find anything. But there was always a chance that a tomb might reward us in the end, and that was always a chance we were willing to take."

So February 8, 1915, should have been a triumphant day for Carter, as what amounted to the pinnacle of his life's work was about to begin.

There was just one problem: *the world was at war.*

All digging in the Valley of the Kings had been stopped. Even worse, orders arrived from the British Army drafting Carter into service.

How dare the venal, tawdry modern world intrude on his search for an ancient king.

Chapter 52

Egyptian Desert
1324 BC

THE BONFIRE LIT UP THE NIGHT, its crackling flames reflecting off the pale tents of Egypt's great army. Tut sat on his traveling throne, with sword-carrying sentries on either side. He was close enough to feel the fire's warmth but distant enough that he was safe from any drunken soldier who might suddenly decide to settle a grudge with the pharaoh.

Tonight such a confrontation was unlikely. The men were beyond euphoric after slaughtering a hated enemy. Blood still flecked many of their faces; desert grime ringed their eyes.

Tut had drunk more wine than was prudent, but he

didn't feel it that much. As he strapped a cloak about
his shoulders to stave off the cold night air, Tut sensed
the men watching him. He detected a new respect.
Their eyes said that today, on the field of battle, he had
behaved as a true king.

Women also ringed the fire, some of them quite beautiful. Several were camp followers who had endured the
long trek from Thebes. But many were captured enemy
women—the prettiest ones—bound at the wrists after
having been dragged from their homes. Their faces
were masks of terror, shame, and loss. They had already
seen their husbands and sons slain. Now, once the fire
died, they would be passed from man to man—a fate
that made many wish that they had died too. Soon, a
few would get their wish and go to the afterworld.

Tut felt one of the women gazing at him. Across the
fire sat a solitary maiden with the most beautiful hair.
Someone's daughter, thought Tut. She was his age, perhaps younger. Raven hair flowed down her back. Dark
brown eyes. Full lips and a strong chin.

His stomach felt funny, a sensation that he at first
blamed on the wine. But now he knew it was nerves,
the same insecurity that had threatened to paralyze
him before battle. Tut shrugged it off and turned away
from the gorgeous girl who dared to stare at him. He
forced himself to think of Ankhesenpaaten, who was
pregnant with their second child. His queen, his lover,
his friend since childhood.

But then Tut found himself staring at the female prisoner. The girl looked even more desirable than before, tossing the ringlets of her hair to better show her profile. If she would have to submit to an Egyptian, she clearly preferred to spend the night with a pharaoh.

He watched as the woman stood, the firelight revealing the sort of full-breasted figure that he had long coveted. Her skirt rode high on her thighs, leaving Tut's imagination free to wander, which it did. How could it not? He was far from home and had just won a great battle.

I am the pharaoh, Tut reminded himself. *What does it matter what others think? Let my wife be angry with me. My father had lovers. So did my father's father, and his father before him. What does it matter if I take this woman to my bed—or take her for my wife, for that matter?*

Tut moved forward until he was sitting on the edge of his seat. By the look in her eye, it was clear that the girl sensed that she was about to be beckoned. Her hard look had softened.

Tut rose and stared at her. He could feel a deep and powerful longing. He studied the girl—her face, lips, every curve—and then he turned and walked to his tent.

Alone.

He remained faithful to Ankhe.

Chapter 53

Tut's Palace
1324 BC

ANKHESENPAATEN STAGGERED into the throne room holding her bulging belly in both hands. She was six months into her second pregnancy.

Each morning she had said a quiet prayer to Amun that this time he would let the baby live. Those prayers had been answered so far, but now something was happening, something new that had her terrified.

"Tut," she whispered from the doorway. "Tut, please."

Tut's advisers stood in a semicircle before his throne, midway through their morning discussion about an upcoming invasion of Nubia. The pharaoh wore just a royal kilt and a decorative collar, for it was summer in Thebes, and at midmorning the temperature was already stifling. When Tut had decided to move the capital back to Thebes, he had not anticipated such extremes of weather.

At the sound of Ankhesenpaaten's voice his head turned toward the doorway. Then he walked quickly to his queen, not caring that his advisers might disapprove.

"What is it, Ankhe?" he asked. After he had returned from war, the two of them had become closer than ever.

"Tut, I can't feel anything."

Tut glanced back at his advisers who were trying — and failing — to pretend that they weren't somehow smug about the conversation.

"I'm sure the baby is just sleeping," Tut said in a low voice.

Ankhesenpaaten shook her head. "It's been a whole day. Usually he moves inside me all the time. Here," she said, taking Tut's hand and placing it against the curve of her abdomen. "Feel that?"

Tut nodded. "That's his foot," she told him. "He normally kicks all the time, but that foot hasn't moved today."

She suddenly gasped in pain and crumpled to the floor. The advisers rushed to the pharaoh and his queen.

"Guard!" Aye yelled. "Send for the royal physician."

Chapter 54

Tut's Palace
1324 BC

ANKHESENPAATEN'S FACE HAD TURNED a sickly shade of pale. She cried out as wave after wave of excruciating pain coursed through her body.

"What is it?" asked Tut, holding her hand tightly. "What is happening?"

"The baby is coming, Tut. Right now."

And at those words, Ankhesenpaaten began to cry. She knew that no child should enter the world so early in a pregnancy. There was no way it would live.

It was as if Tut and his advisers did not exist now. Alone with the child, she curled into a ball on the floor and sobbed bitterly, pressing her face into the cool, smooth stone.

"I am so ashamed," she whispered.

"My queen..." said Tut.

"I am not worthy of being called your queen," she said, sitting up straight and looking deeply into Tut's eyes. The bile in her throat rose as she stared at the three advisers. "I cannot give you an heir. Don't you see? I am incapable."

The advisers said nothing to this, but none would have disagreed. Thanks to their spies within the royal household, the aging men knew that she referred to them as the Serpents. The girl was arrogant and disrespectful, but she was also very smart.

"Don't speak nonsense," Tut said in an unconvincing voice. This was the moment he had feared since Ankhesenpaaten had announced that she was with child again. "We'll put the child in my burial tomb. Much of it is already finished."

"You're not listening to me," said Ankhesenpaaten, just as a contraction sent a new wave of pain through her body.

"She's right," Horemheb pronounced. "She sees things clearly."

Tut got to his feet and stood toe to toe with the general. "Do you dare tell the pharaoh that he is in error?"

Horemheb didn't back down all the way. "No, sir. I

am merely agreeing with your queen. You heard her. She is telling you to take another wife. Listen to her."

Tut bent to the floor and scooped up Ankhesen-paaten. Lovingly, he kissed her cheek as she wrapped her arms around his neck and he carried her to the royal bedroom.

"I will deal with you later," Tut said to Horemheb. "Egypt is a land of many generals. Do not forget it."

Then, to Aye, he added, "Send the doctor to the bed-room. Do it quickly, Scribe."

Chapter 55

Tut's Palace
1324 BC

TUT STRIPPED DOWN at his bedside, letting his kilt
fall to the floor for a servant to clean in the morning.

He took off his eye paint, which was black, and
extended to his temples. He rinsed his mouth from a
tumbler of water on the nightstand, then slid into bed.
The pillow was cool against his bare, shaved head, and
the cotton sheets gently caressed his torso. Like most
Egyptians, he was obsessed with hygiene and cleanli-
ness. The hair on his body was regularly removed with
razors and clippers.

Now he lay back and wondered what would happen
next.

All night long the palace had been buzzing about the angry confrontation between Aye and the pharaoh. Tut could feel it in the way the servants brought his dinner, keeping their eyes more downcast than usual.

"Egypt is once again powerful and prosperous," the royal vizier had bellowed. "This is due to me, Pharaoh. Not you. Not your queen. Your father ran this country nearly into ruin, and I have built it up again. Now you threaten all we have worked for by not producing an heir."

The vizier continued: "This thing you two call 'love' is a greater threat to Egypt than the Canaanites, the Nubians, and all our other neighbors. And yet you revel in your cozy affections. You rub our noses in it. These people"—now Aye threw his arm out toward the city—"deserve a pharaoh who puts the nation first."

"I am pharaoh. I can do whatever I want to do. You are but a man, Scribe."

As Tut entered his bedroom alone, after seeing Ankhesenpaaten to her room, he was aware that every person in the palace waited to see what would happen next.

Would Aye make good on his promise to bring a handmaiden to Tut's bed?

At midnight, with the full moon pouring into his open window, Tut got his answer. He heard two sets of footsteps in the corridor outside. The first was heavy and labored and the other soft.

Then came a delicate rustle as the lighter footsteps tiptoed into his room. Tut could sense hesitation, perhaps fear, as the feet came closer and closer to his bed. He could almost feel the pounding of the young girl's heart.

What must she be thinking, Tut wondered, lying flat on his back, his eyes still adjusting to the near darkness. *She has come to have sex with the pharaoh. Of course she is a virgin, so the mere act of making love is mysterious and frightening.*

But to lie down with the ruler of all Egypt? With me?

Tut rolled onto his side to have a look. His fierce loyalty to his queen almost caused him to send the girl away, but he had held back for the moment, though he was unsure why.

Now he saw her.

The girl looked to be sixteen or seventeen. Tut remembered admiring her at a state dinner and thinking she might be the daughter of a local dignitary. That she was a great beauty, there was no doubt. She stood at the side of the bed, very demure, moonlight shining through her sheer robe. Tut was mesmerized at the sight of her: her shape, her long black hair, her dark eyes still painted. Her perfume was a pleasing combination of lemon and flowers.

"What is your name?" he said softly, surprised to feel the beating of his own heart, surprised that he cared about her feelings.

"Tuya," she whispered.

"Take off your robe, Tuya. Don't be afraid. There's no need of that. Not here."

Tuya did as she was told, pulling the fabric from her shoulders, letting it drop to the floor.

"Turn around for me. Slowly. You're very beautiful. Please, don't be fearful."

She spun in a circle, her shoulders back and head held high. Then she took a tentative step toward him.

"Wait," Tut said, seized by a sudden image of Ankhesenpaaten. What was his queen doing now? And what would she say if she could see him? How would this affect their love—what Aye had called "cozy affection"?

Tuya stopped and self-consciously placed her hands over her breasts.

Tut got out of bed then and walked to her. Her eyes grew wide at the sight of him, which only increased his arousal.

Next, he kissed Tuya's lips and found them to be soft, even more so than Ankhe's. Her breath was fresh and sweet, and she hungrily thrust her tongue into his mouth.

The young pharaoh didn't think of his queen for the rest of that long sleepless night.

Chapter 56

Tut's Palace
1324 BC

ANKHESENPAATEN COULDN'T SLEEP. The mere thought of what was happening in Tut's bedroom filled her with jealousy and more than a little sadness. From the time they were children, she had always loved Tut. And the men in the palace had always gotten in the way.

She stood and slipped on a robe, then walked quietly outside into the gardens. The air was cold, and she shivered from the chill. There was much on her mind. She thought of Tut again and that girl and then quickly banished the image.

He's not enjoying it, she assured herself.

Oh, yes he is, shot back an inner voice.

That night at dinner she'd overheard the servants laughing at her, scornful that a queen was incapable of bringing children into the world.

Yes, I can! She'd wanted to scream. *I have brought two wonderful children into this world. The gods have seen fit to send them to the afterworld, but I will bear more.*

Why does no one point the finger at Tut?

Why does he not endure the pain of childbirth, only to have the infant perish? Why is he allowed to take a woman to his bed to produce an heir, while I am left here alone? What if I felt like taking a man to my bed? What then? Maybe I do feel like it sometimes.

She stood and paced. The queen was barefoot, and the path had many small pebbles that dug into the soles of her feet, causing her to step gingerly. One sharp stone made her stop completely. Yet she reveled in the petty annoyance. *This is nothing like childbirth, Tut! That was pain!*

She considered racing to the other side of the palace and confronting the lovers, all tangled and sweaty in his bed.

You told him to do it, she reminded herself.

Yes, but I didn't mean it.

She would march in and claw the girl's face until her beauty was gone forever. And then she would strike out at Tut.

No, I can't do that. I do love him. He is my king, the king of all of Egypt.

192

But he abandoned you. He is in another woman's arms this very minute. They are speaking intimate words— whispering and laughing and touching one another. That's treason, in its own way. Why shouldn't he die?

He is a pharaoh, and pharaohs have harems. This is just one girl.

But we promised each other. We promised to be true.

He would kill me if I broke that promise.

No, he wouldn't. He may never touch you again. But he wouldn't kill you.

It doesn't matter. I could do it. A simple thrust with a knife is all it would take.

Be smart about this. Take a breath and think.

I am the queen. I am the woman of full noble birth. It was through marriage to me that Tut gained his throne.

I can do the same with another man. Just watch me.

Chapter 57

Tut's Palace
1324 BC

"IT'S *YOU*, PHARAOH." Aye smirked, and nobody in the palace could smirk like Aye.

They marched side by side to the royal stables, the air smelling of manure and sweet green alfalfa. Tut was already late for his chariot ride.

Tuya had kept him up all night again, and rather than sleep the day away he was determined to revive himself with a hard gallop across the desert on the east side of the Nile. In truth, he was troubled and confused—about Tuya—and about Ankhesenpaaten.

"What are you talking about?" he said. "Your words are a muddle."

"Tuya is not with child. The problem is not her, pharaoh, and it is not your queen. You are the reason there is no royal heir. *It's you!*"

Tut flushed angrily. "That is not possible! My manhood is beyond question."

He had reached his chariot and now grabbed the reins from a young stable boy. The horses lifted their heads from a trough of alfalfa and whinnied in anticipation.

"From the looks of things, there are no arrows in your quiver," continued Aye.

That was the last straw. "Guards," commanded Tut. "*Seize him.*"

The contingent of six royal guards moved forward and towered over Aye, yet they were apprehensive, as if looking to Aye for leadership rather than Tut.

"*Now!*" Tut screamed, rage and humiliation pouring through. He was the pharaoh. He could impregnate every virgin in Egypt if he wished. It wasn't his fault that Tuya was having trouble bearing a child. Maybe Aye had chosen her because she was known to be infertile, all part of his scheme.

Aye didn't struggle as the guards clamped their hands on his arms and shoulders. No—all he did was smirk.

"I am the pharaoh, Aye. You will remember that from now on." Tut stepped into his chariot.

"I am going for a ride," he told the captain of the

guards, a Nubian with huge biceps. "By the time I return, you will have administered fifty lashes to the royal vizier. Am I understood?"

The smirk was gone from Aye's face now, much to Tut's delight. "As you wish, Pharaoh," Aye muttered in supplication, "so it shall be." Even ten lashes would have been too much. Fifty would lay Aye's back open to the bone and leave permanent scars that would be a brand of shame for the rest of his life.

For just an instant, Tut thought that Aye's tone was sincere, and he considered rescinding the punishment. But the defiant look in the vizier's eyes was still there, and Tut sensed the humility was an act.

With a final glare, Tut whipped his reins and raced across the desert.

Chapter 58

Egyptian Desert
1324 BC

THE FORGIVING ELM wheels of the chassis provided the only shock absorption, but the terrain was smooth and so was the ride.

A lone man atop a camel could be seen in the distance, but otherwise Tut had the desert to himself, as he liked it.

Within a few minutes, his forehead was sweating, and the dust from the horse's hooves covered his chest. This was what he loved, but today even a fast chariot ride didn't help.

Tut was so caught up in thoughts of Aye's insolence and his own inability to produce an heir that he didn't notice that the desert had become more rugged in the few miles since his journey began.

And he didn't see the deep cleft that had probably been created by a flash flood.

That is, not until it was too late to avoid it.

Hitting the rut, Tut was thrown headfirst from the chariot. He landed hard on the ground and was knocked unconscious for a time.

He came to slowly, moaning, and found himself staring up at the face of...*a camel.*

The rider was kneeling over Tut, checking for signs of injury, clearly unaware that the man before him was Egypt's pharaoh.

Instead, the robber—and that's what he was, Tut now realized—relieved the pharaoh of the expensive floral collar, then frisked the royal body for money.

Tut would have told the man who he was, except that—strangely—he seemed unable to utter a word.

Only when the man was sure that Tut wasn't carrying a purse did he leave but not before stealing Tut's sandals and kilt.

Night was falling as Tut faded back into unconsciousness.

Chapter 59

Tut's Palace
1324 BC

"WE NEED TO TALK."

"I'm listening."

It was an hour before dawn. The entire palace was astir. After the largest manhunt in Egyptian history, the pharaoh had been located in the desert west of Thebes. Tut had been robbed of all his possessions, no doubt by a nomad. The young pharaoh was still unconscious.

In addition to a high fever, his body was covered with bruises and abrasions. Now Aye and Horemheb stood on opposite sides of his bed, looking down at their comatose ruler. The cavernous bedroom was dark, save for the moonlight shining in the window.

Aye said, "We should take this conversation into the hall."

Horemheb pursed his lips. A long straight scar ran diagonally across his face, the result of a Hittite sword. When he was tense, it took on a reddish hue that made it stand out, even against his sun-damaged skin.

"If we go anywhere else, we will be observed. Obviously, the pharaoh cannot hear us. It's better if we talk here."

Aye didn't like to be contradicted, but Horemheb was probably right. Besides, the royal vizier was still in great pain after enduring the humiliating lashes Tut had ordered. The guards had gone easy on him because of his status, but a few of the lashes had sliced into his skin. Now his back was a swollen mess, oozing blood and crisscrossed with whip marks.

"All right. Here then," said Aye. He glanced about the room to make sure no one was there to overhear them. "I am getting to be an old man. I have served my nation since I was an adolescent and learned the serpentine ways of the royal court. We both witnessed the ruin brought on by Akhenaten's reign, and we know that Tut is moving too slowly to fix the damage."

"Are you saying—"

"Yes," Aye stated flatly. "And if you help me, I can ensure that you will be my successor. I will not live long, but in my short time as pharaoh I can return Egypt to her former glory. You will complete the task, General."

Horemheb's scar was now a vibrant magenta. "How would we do this? Look at him. He's a boy. No doubt he'll recover from his fall."

Horemheb sighed. He was nervous, yet he reveled in the notion of being pharaoh. "I never thought the day would come that I would speak openly... of killing the pharaoh."

Before Aye could respond, they heard sandals shuffling on the tiled floor. They turned to face the sound, and Horemheb instinctively moved to block the door.

"Show yourself," said Aye. "Come out now. Who's there? *Who?*"

Yuye, the queen's lady-in-waiting, a tall girl with green eyes, stepped out of the shadows. She was just a teenager, and the palace knew her as Ankhesenpaaten's confidante. If anyone would tell the queen of their discussion, she would.

The girl was clearly terrified. "I didn't hear anything, Vizier."

"Yes, you did."

Horemheb took a step toward Yuye. His hand was up, ready to slap her. But Aye stopped him.

"You'll leave a mark," he said to the general. "We don't want that, do we?"

Aye turned his attention to Yuye. "The issue is not whether you *heard* something, but whether you will *say* something."

"I won't. I promise I won't."

Aye grabbed the girl's wrist and yanked her toward him. His face was just inches from hers as he issued a quiet threat: "I know."

Aye then turned to Horemheb. "You think of a plan for him," he said, nodding his head in the direction of Tut, "I'll take care of the girl."

Chapter 60

Tut's Palace
1324 BC

AT FIRST YUYE WAS CERTAIN Aye was going to kill her and dispose of her body. He'd forcibly pulled her out of Tut's bedroom, his grip so tight that she thought her wrist might break.

There was a bedroom two doors down, and he led her inside. Then he threw her down on the bed.

"The queen will find out if you kill me," she said, sounding bolder than she felt.

"I know," Aye said simply. Then he completely surprised Yuye. He told her to take off her clothes.

He did the same.

Now the aging vizier was on top of her. Yuye was not a virgin, but she hadn't had much experience either. She didn't know what she was expected to do, but she did know that if she cried out for help she would probably die. Maybe not tonight. Maybe not tomorrow. So she submitted.

What choice did she have? Aye was the supreme legal official in Egypt. Only the pharaoh could overrule him. Aye, in other words, was the law. He, and he alone, decided what constituted rape.

At least he didn't use force, so Yuye simply endured, knowing that this was one secret she could never tell the queen.

Aye seemed close to finishing, when suddenly he stopped himself and became talkative. "Listen to me. You will be my spy. Do you agree to do this?"

"I don't understand. What kind of spy?"

"You will tell me the queen's secrets. *That* kind of spy."

"She will become suspicious. She is no one's fool."

Aye was quiet for a moment. The muscles of his still-raw backside clenched, and he arched his back.

Then he raised his fist and brought it down hard into the girl's ribs. It was more pain than Yuye had ever felt in her life. She couldn't breathe to cry out.

Now Aye rolled off her. "There will be more of this—more of us. I'll let you know when and where.

In the meantime, anything and everything that comes from the queen's lips will be reported to me. Am I understood?"

Yuye nodded. Of course she understood.

Then Aye rolled back on top of the girl.

Chapter 61

Tut's Palace
1324 BC

IT HAD BEEN a week since the pharaoh's chariot accident. Tut was well enough to sit up and take broth and sip a glass of wine that contained powdered eggshells, which the physicians believed would help heal the shell of Tut's head.

But for the most part Tut slept, his every toss and turn watched by Tuya and the queen. The two women took turns attending him. Ankhesenpaaten had decided that they would be the ones to nurse him back to health.

Ankhe dabbed his forehead with a cool cloth, then bent down to tenderly kiss him. He had spoken a few words to her earlier, but she knew he wasn't safe yet.

The wounds would heal eventually, but his infections could worsen. She had seen this happen many times with the sick.

She kissed him again and then whispered, "I forgive you." She believed that she did. Tut had been unfaithful but for the good of Egypt and only as a last resort. Most important, it had been her idea.

The queen stood up and smoothed her dress, leaving Tut to sleep.

Now Tut lay alone in the darkness, breathing softly. She had left the white cloth on his forehead but otherwise his skull was uncovered. *Was he healing?* the queen wondered.

It was well past dark as she made her way back to her side of the palace. She was drowsy after a long day caring for the ailing pharaoh.

Suddenly, a sound echoed down the hallway. "Who's there?" she asked. "I heard someone."

There was no answer, so the queen continued to her room.

A moment after she passed, a bulky figure stepped out from behind one of several stone statues that decorated the hall. Quickly, quietly, the man went into Tut's room and hurried toward the pharaoh's bed.

In his hand, a two-foot-long club. In his heart, murder.

Chapter 62

Valley of the Kings
1917

LIKE A GENERAL COMMANDING a small army, Carter barked orders, positioning his workers across the landscape in the spots where they would soon dig and dig, then dig some more.

The men marched to their positions and leaned on their hoe-like *turias*, knowing that the work would not commence until Carter said so.

The forty-three-year-old Howard Carter, fluent in Arabic and knowledgeable about Egypt, had been deemed a vital resource by the British Army. So, rather than searching for forgotten pharaohs, he'd spent the war in Cairo, laboring for the Military Intelligence Department of the War Office.

"War work claimed most of my time for the next few years," he wrote, "but there were occasional intervals when I was able to carry out small pieces of excavation."

But those were strictly reconnaissance efforts, not genuine searches for Tut or some other lost pharaoh. Then on December 1, 1917, while war was still being waged in Europe, Carter was finally released from duty and allowed to return to his beloved Valley of the Kings.

"The difficulty was knowing where to begin," he noted. "I suggested to Lord Carnarvon that we take as a starting point the triangle of ground defined by the tombs of Rameses II, Mer-en-Ptah, and Rameses VI."

Just as so many soldiers in the trenches had longed for loved ones, so had Carter pined for the valley. To be standing here beneath the blazing blue skies, feeling a fine layer of dust settle on his skin—it was like falling in love all over again.

"Proceed," he yelled, his words echoing.

The bare-chested army of diggers swung their *turias* into the earth.

Carter intended to clear the area around the tombs of Rameses II and Rameses VI right down to the bedrock, a task that would require removing tens of thousands of tons of stone and soil. He had already laid narrow-gauge tracks and arranged to have a small train haul away that debris.

The plan was ambitious, but after a decade of waiting, anything less would not have been acceptable to Carter or His Lordship. There was too much stored up energy, too much deferred ambition.

But would he find his virgin tomb? Would he find King Tut?

Davis had said that the valley had been exhausted, and by the time he'd up and left, the American had become its leading authority. For that reason experts had taken Davis at his word.

But now Davis was dead, having keeled over from a heart attack just six months after abandoning the valley. Carter, however, was very much alive and hard at work.

He wondered about his diggers, those veterans with calloused hands and broad shoulders who had moved so much earth in their lives. Did they also think the valley was exhausted? Were they just here for the paycheck? Did they believe they were digging all day long in the blazing sun with no hope of finding anything? Or did they believe in their hearts that they might help unearth a long-buried tomb?

Would they discover the elusive Tut?

Chapter 63

Valley of the Kings
1920

BUT TUT'S TOMB would not be found in 1917 or 1918 or 1919, for that matter.

Carter surveyed the Valley of the Kings with deepening frustration and little of his usual quixotic hopefulness.

Hundreds of workers had labored on Lord Carnarvon's payroll for a number of long seasons—and for nothing of any real value. In Luxor, Carter was something of a laughingstock, a sad man tilting at windmills.

Carter had found tombs that had been begun but never finished, caches of alabaster jars, a series of workmen's huts. And though his patience seemed inexhaustible, Lord Carnarvon's was not. "We had now dug in the valley for several seasons with extremely scanty results," Carter lamented. "It had become a much debated question whether we should continue the work or try for a more profitable site elsewhere. After these barren years, were we justified in going on?"

He looked out at the valley, searching for some sign of King Tut. As Carter explained it: "So long as a single area of untouched ground remained, the risk was worth taking." His rationale was simple: "If a lucky strike be made, you will be repaid for years and years of dull and unprofitable work."

His gaze rested on the flint boulders and workmen's huts over by the tomb of Rameses VI.

That would be his focus next year—*if there was to be a next year.*

Chapter 64

Tut's Palace
1324 BC

A SOLITARY FIGURE MOVED like a ghost through the pharaoh's bedroom—an angry, vengeful ghost.

He was a soldier in the Egyptian army, a man named Abdul, who had been conscripted at the age of eight and spent every day since in the service of the pharaoh. He had no wife, no children, and his parents had long since entered the afterworld. This warrior, in essence, was a nobody who had nothing. He had never risen above the rank of foot soldier. On the eve of his fortieth birthday, his left eye had been put out by a Hittite lance, but other than that he had few visible scars to show for a lifetime of war.

Abdul was unused to the finery of the palace. He felt certain that he would be discovered at every turn in the hallway. But he'd only seen the queen leaving Tut's bedroom. It was as if the guards had all been told to take the night off. Had that been arranged too?

He had left his sandals at the barracks, knowing that his feet would be quieter on tile. His chest was bare, and his kilt was a faded blue. He wore nothing on his head, but in his hand he clutched a special implement prepared for him by one of General Horemheb's top weapon makers.

A smooth Nile stone the size of a grapefruit had been tied with leather straps to the end of a two-foot length of polished ebony.

By all appearances, it was a most attractive and suitable war club. Abdul knew, however, that the club was too pretty for combat.

But it would be perfect for murdering a young pharaoh.

Chapter 65

Valley of the Kings
February 26, 1920

A DISCOVERY HAD BEEN MADE, but what kind of discovery was it? Large or small?

Carter bent down to be the first to examine the find. Lord Carnarvon was close on his heels, as was his wife, Lady Carnarvon.

They appeared to be inspecting a common debris pile—rocks, sand, chips of flint and pottery tossed aside during the excavation of a tomb long ago.

But peeking out, smooth and white, were alabaster jars—a dozen or more.

And the jars were intact.

Carter stepped forward to clear away more dirt, but

the normally reserved Lady Carnarvon beat him to it. Though heavyset and past her prime, she dropped down to her knees and clawed fitfully at the soil. The Carnarvons had invested substantial time and money in the valley, and this was the first significant treasure they had to show for it. Lady Carnarvon would not be denied the opportunity to enjoy the discovery every bit as much as the men.

Carter and the workers stood back to watch as she cleared the soil away from each jar.

A tally was taken when she was done: thirteen. Perfect and near pristine, they were most certainly related to the burial of a king named Merenptah and represented a decent find.

There were, however, no markings indicating that the jars had anything to do with Tut. As minor as the find may have been, something was better than nothing. And with the close of the 1920 dig season just a week off, it would end the period of labor on a high note.

"It was the nearest approach to a real find that we had yet made in the valley," Carter wrote in his journal.

Once again, he was the hopeful Don Quixote of Egypt.

Chapter 66

Highclere Castle near Newbury, England
1922

TO BE HONEST, Carter's time in the valley had been expensive and fruitless. He had found nothing to warrant the hundreds of thousands of pounds Lord Carnarvon had spent in search of a great lost pharaoh — or even a minor one.

The alabaster jars had buoyed hope after the 1920 season, momentarily pushing aside memories of barren searches in years past.

But 1921 had yielded nothing important. There seemed no reason to think that the upcoming 1922 season would be any different.

Now the two men strolled across the sprawling

grounds of Highclere Castle, Carnarvon's family estate back in England.

The mood was uneasy, and Carter had an inkling that he had been summoned for very bad news.

The two had become unlikely friends over the years. They had spent so much time together, fingers crossed, praying that their next effort would be the one to unearth some great buried treasure. But now that hope was apparently gone.

Tons of rock had been scraped away. But Howard Carter hadn't made a major find in almost twenty years, and his reputation as a cranky, self-important, washed-up Egyptologist was well known in Luxor and even here in England.

The war hadn't helped. His Lordship's health had suffered in the absence of those warm Egyptian winters. He had gotten out of the habit, so to speak. And now he was ready to stop funding costly excavations that yielded nothing.

Carter quietly made his case anyway: He had located ancient workmen's huts near the tomb of Rameses VI, but because of heavy tourist traffic he hadn't been able to dig deeper. His plan was to start digging *in early November* to avoid the peak tourist season.

Carnarvon rebuffed him. He was through with the valley. There would be no more excavations with his money. Their partnership was over. "I'm so sorry, Howard. I'm nearly as sad about this as you are," Carnarvon said.

The news would have been even more crushing to Carter if he had not anticipated this moment and planned his next move. He cleared his throat. "There's one last tomb to be found, sir. I'm sure of it. So sure that, if you will allow me to make use of your concession in the valley, I will fund the next year of digging myself. Of course," he added hastily, "we would split whatever I find evenly."

Carnarvon was astounded. "You don't have that kind of money," he exclaimed

"I'll find the money, sir."

"You will? To pay the wages of a hundred diggers? To pay for the guards? To feed yourself?"

Carter offered a rare smile. "I'm not all that hungry, for food that is. I suppose I will need cigarette money."

Carnarvon squinted as he rubbed a manicured hand across his face. He was touched by this show of faith. "I will fund one more year. But just one, Howard. This is your last chance. Find King Tut, or we're done."

Part Three

Chapter 67

Palm Beach, Florida
Present Day

"WHAT ARE YOU SMILING ABOUT, Jim?" asked Susan. My wife was standing in the doorway to my office. She's tall and blonde, like a femme fatale from a forties film noir—though a femme fatale from Wisconsin.

I had just hung up the phone—with Marty Dugard, actually. "My gut feeling is getting stronger. Tut was murdered, Sue. I just have to figure out who killed the poor guy."

"A hunch doesn't mean very much if you can't prove it," she said. "Am I missing something?"

"Oh, I'll prove it," I said with a grin. "And thanks for the vote of confidence."

"Anytime," she called over her shoulder. Femme fatale? Definitely.

Sue had a point though. How was I going to prove that Tut hadn't died from wounds suffered in his chariot crash? That was the most widely accepted theory about his death.

My most popular fictional character, Dr. Alex Cross, lives by his hunches and instincts. Quite possibly that's because I do as well. At that moment, I felt I was gathering evidence that Tut had been murdered and that I would soon know who was responsible for Tut's death —perhaps someone you might not expect. *That* was what had me excited now.

I had been making notes on a new Cross manuscript before the call from Marty Dugard. The pages were stacked in a pile on my desk, next to pages from a dozen other projects I had in the works.

That's pretty much the way of my workday: up at 5:00 a.m., write and edit, take a break—maybe golf, maybe a movie—then get back to it. Seven days a week. I have an ability, or a curse, to focus on several projects at once. But Tut was distracting me from all the other projects.

Ignoring the Cross manuscript, I reached for my list of pharaohs.

The New Kingdom, as the era spanning the Eighteenth to Twentieth Dynasties was known, had lasted a little more than five hundred years. There were thirty-two pharaohs during that time, but the ones I was interested in were Tut and the man who succeeded him. It seemed reasonable to presume that the person who had the most to gain by Tut's death was the man ascending to the throne after him. Follow the money, follow the power.

I ran my finger down the list. Right then, a gust of wind blew in through the open window, scattering part of the Cross manuscript on the floor. I half wondered whether some ancient Egyptian god had been responsible for that. Or was it part of the pharaoh's curse?

I read the succession of kings out loud. "Amenhotep II, Tuthmosis IV, Amenhotep III, Akhenaten, Nefertiti, Tutankhamen..."

Then I stopped.

Not just the next name but the next *two* names held my attention. I had looked at this roster before, but only now was I beginning to realize what it could mean. These weren't only names—they were pieces of a puzzle that hadn't been solved for thousands of years.

Staring at them, I began to think that I wasn't studying a random act of murder but a cold-blooded conspiracy. There was that gut instinct of mine again—the reason, I think, that *Time* magazine had once called me "The Man Who Can't Miss."

We'd see about that soon, wouldn't we?

Chapter 68

Valley of the Kings
November 1, 1922

THE MEN WERE ASSEMBLED for work, usually a twelve-hour day, sunrise to sunset. Carter knew most of them by name or sight after working the valley year after year. They carried their digging tools casually over their shoulders and wore thin sandals and flowing white shirts that extended to their ankles.

"*Mabrook*," they called out in greeting, their smiles a sure sign that they were ready for a brand-new season with their demanding boss man.

Carter tried to appear upbeat, but now even he was racked by self-doubt.

"We had now dug in the valley for several seasons

with extremely scanty results," he wrote in a rare candid moment. "After these barren years, were we justified going on with it?"

He had decided that they were and had convinced Lord Carnarvon to wager another several thousand pounds. Nodding to his foreman, Reis Ahmed Gerigar, Carter gave the official order to start.

They were beginning two months earlier than usual, hoping to finish their work before the tourist season began.

Near where he stood, just in front of the cavernous opening to the tomb of Rameses VI, rose a triangle of ruins first excavated five years earlier—a chain of ancient workmen's huts.

"They were probably used by the laborers in the tomb of Rameses. These huts, built about three feet above bedrock, covered the whole area in front of the Ramesside tomb and continued in a southerly direction to join up with a similar group of huts on the opposite side of the valley, discovered by Davis in connection with his work on the Akhenaten cache," Carter noted dutifully.

First, Carter's men would record the precise location and dimensions of each hut. Then they would remove the huts and dig down through the soil to the bedrock.

Only when they struck bedrock could they begin stripping away the remaining sand and dirt to search for the seam in the earth that might lead to Tut and his tomb. A tomb architect would have cut straight down into the rock to create the most solid and long-lasting burial place imaginable. There would be a descending staircase perhaps or a long-buried passageway to mark the opening.

Or so Carter hoped.

He peered closely at the earth to reassure himself. Beneath the stone huts stood three feet of loose rock and sand, the former, courtesy of the slaves and prisoners who had carved the tomb of Rameses VI. This was where stone chipped from inside the tomb had been dumped. The sand came courtesy of a landslide.

"I had always had a kind of superstitious feeling that in that particular corner of the valley one of the missing kings, possibly Tutankhamen, might be found," Carter wrote in a journal that could have filled several books like this one.

But a strong gut feeling was all he had to go on. Certainly, this was the very last part of the valley that had not been fully explored. But who could say if or when another lost treasure would be found.

Carter fell into the habit of watching the men working. They talked nonstop, gossiping about their friends and wives as their *turias* dug into the rocky soil. The tools clanked when hitting rock, and the work had a cadence that was almost musical to Carter's ear.

Despite their chattiness, his men were deliberate

228

and precise. Years of toil in the valley had made them proficient Egyptologists in their own right. They knew when to proceed cautiously and when to move earth with abandon.

So there was little for Carter to do but stand and watch and hope this would be his year. No matter how fast his crew moved, excavating down to the bed-rock would take days. He thought it might be better to return home, get out of the sun, and unpack the food and wine that had just arrived from London.

But he stayed on at the site anyway, preferring to endure what he called the creeping "doubts, born of previous disappointments" there than at his home.

He lit another cigarette and watched the dirt fly.

Chapter 69

Valley of the Kings
November 4, 1922

IT WAS DAWN, three days into the season. Thus far nothing had been found, and there seemed to be no particular reason to hope that anything would be found.

The first day's optimism had already given way to grumbling and low morale. The diggers were still chatty but seemed subdued and disappointed, almost as if they had already given up.

A young boy, a worker's son, played happily in the loose sand. His job was to tote water, but the sun wasn't high enough yet for the men to be thirsty, so he contented himself by pretending to be one of the diggers.

The boy knew to keep away from the ancient

workmen's huts where the men dug, so he dug into the ground nearby with a pair of sticks he had carried from home early that morning.

The sand was fine and not at all hard. It didn't take much effort for him to plunge his sticks into the ground.

One stick hit something solid! His heart beat a little faster as he began wondering what it might be. He dropped his stick and started to use his hands to push back the soil.

The boy looked around to see if anyone had noticed him. He was fearful that someone would see him digging and take credit for whatever he had discovered.

A solid object soon revealed itself. It was flat and smooth and made of stone. The more dirt he cleared away, the more the boy could see that the object was something very worthwhile indeed.

It was a step.

Here, not where the men were digging.

Someone long ago had carved the step out of bedrock. Time and the elements had covered it over until this young water boy, thousands of years later, reclaimed it from the earth with a pair of twigs.

The boy looked around again, making sure no one had seen him.

Quickly, he pulled the sand back into the hole and carefully marked the spot. Then he ran off to tell Mr. Howard Carter about the mysterious stairway.

Chapter 70

Egyptian Desert

1324 BC

"HALT THE EXCAVATION!"

The voice echoed down the corridor above the din of hammering and chipping.

The overseer was furious. No one but the pharaoh could issue such an order.

He planted his feet, placed one calloused hand on each hip, and turned to glare at this offensive idiot, whomever he might be.

He heard footsteps slapping down the corridor, then the angry cries of workmen who were being trampled on by the interloper. Of course, they were prisoners of war and petty criminals who would be executed when the job was finished to keep the tomb's location a secret. He cared little that they were inconvenienced.

A royal page skittered to a halt directly in front of the overseer. He wore a fashionable kilt and an extra-heavy application of eyeliner that had begun to run in the heat.

The overseer believed that the man worked for the royal vizier, though he wasn't certain. Either way, it was best to keep his temper in check. He forced himself to count to ten, lest he smack the man across his arrogant face.

"By what right do you barge into my construction site and issue such a decree?" the overseer said in measured syllables.

"By order of the royal vizier," replied the page.

The overseer calmed down a little. "I'm listening. By order of the vizier, *what?*"

"The pharaoh is dead." The page leaned forward and whispered in a voice so low that the overseer could barely hear. "There are rumors that he has been murdered and that more deaths will follow."

The overseer's shock was evident, which pleased the gossipy page. "Is this a secret?" asked the overseer.

"The biggest. If I were you, I would not repeat it."

"You just did."

"You are not me, grave digger."

There was a moment of strained silence. The overseer was so consumed with the astounding news that it took a moment for the ramifications to settle in.

"I can't finish this tomb in seventy days," he said, alluding to the prescribed mourning, embalming, and mummification period before a pharaoh would be sealed inside the ground for eternity. "It is impossible."

"That is why I have come. We will finish *this* tomb later. The pharaoh will be buried in the tomb at the center of the valley."

The overseer was once again astonished. "That is no tomb for a pharaoh. It is a trifle. Just four rooms and the narrowest of hallways. It is a closet!"

"Yes, but it is a finished closet."

"It still needs to be painted," replied the overseer, trying to maintain some control over the situation. It was customary to paint scenes from the pharaoh's life and his journey into the afterworld on the walls in vivid colors.

"Exactly. You had better get your men painting pretty pictures."

"Stop the excavation!" roared the overseer. He paused, and then looked at the page curiously.

"Who will—"

"Inherit this tomb?" answered the page, anticipating the words.

The overseer nodded.

"The Royal Vizier has graciously offered to take it off the pharaoh's hands."

Chapter 71

Valley of the Kings
1324 BC

ANKHESENPAATEN STOOD ATOP the stone steps that led down into her husband's tomb. The funeral was more than two months away, but she wanted to see for herself where he would rest for eternity.

The mummies of their dead children would be interred here too. But she was destined to be far away, in the Valley of the Queens. The thought of that separation filled her with grief, even though she knew they would meet again in the afterlife.

She nodded to Yuye, her lady-in-waiting, signaling that she did not want to be followed. Then the queen descended the steps.

The steps led to a hallway, the floor of which dipped gently into the earth. She noted with disappointment the lack of decoration, the walls of bare rock.

Ankhesenpaaten understood that time was short. Still, a few simple paintings would have been better and more fitting.

She turned back toward the light at the tomb entrance, checking to see if she had been followed. There was no sign of anyone.

Ankhesenpaaten breathed a sigh of relief. More than anything, she wanted to be alone right now. She had much to think about.

The hallway led into a large chamber, and a slightly smaller room lay beyond that. The way was lit by small lamps whose ghostly flickerings danced on the walls.

The queen was heartened when she finally gazed upon murals depicting Tut's life. At least he would be remembered here.

In the center of the small room was Tut's throne, as if waiting for him to arrive. She walked to it, running her hand along the wood.

Ankhesenpaaten smiled as she examined the back of the chair, where scenes of their life together had been carved. There was one of her anointing him with oil. And another of them hunting together, his bow at the ready as she handed him an arrow and pointed to a fat Nile duck.

She remembered the day, or one exactly like it, as if it were yesterday.

There was another reason she'd come here: Ankhesenpaaten was terrified for her own life.

She circled the throne, afraid of the emotions welling up inside her. She had never felt so alone before, had never so needed of Tut's reassuring voice. He would know what to do. She had seen him grow more and more confident in Aye's presence, so much so that Aye had little or no power over him.

Tut had been fond of reminding her that Aye and his wife had been little more than glorified servants to their parents. Indeed, Aye's wife had been Nefertiti's wet-nurse. The queen had nothing to fear from them.

Ankhesenpaaten took a deep breath, then allowed herself to settle onto the throne. She sat up straight at first, then settled back until she was relaxed in the chair. That was how Tut sat there, not erect, like some tentative ruler, but slumped and secure.

She could almost hear his voice as she sat there. He would be speaking directly, unafraid to tell the truth to whomever needed to hear it.

Ankhesenpaaten felt power rising within her, as if Tut himself were giving her confidence. But it was too much. She broke down in tears, sobbing alone in the tomb.

Tut was gone from this world; there was no getting around it. How would she rule without him?

His voice came to her, strong and sure: *A woman cannot be pharaoh these days. You have two choices—*

either marry Aye and let him rule, or find a foreign king to occupy the throne. Some of her sisters had married Asians. Why should she be different?

Because they were princesses, and I am the queen—and right now the pharaoh too.

Ankhesenpaaten stopped crying, but the grief in her heart was great. She didn't want to marry anyone else and certainly not Aye. But she was the queen, and she had no choice. Whatever plan she followed, it must be for the good of Egypt.

The queen gazed at the walls again. It was amazing to think that his body would be sealed inside this very room, forever. She desperately wanted to share this chamber with him.

But she couldn't worry about that right now. She needed to act quickly.

Ankhesenpaaten strode from the burial chamber, shoulders back and head high. In her mind she was already composing the letter that might set her free.

Or possibly get her killed—just like poor Tut.

Chapter 72

Valley of the Kings
April 1324 BC

EGYPT'S WEALTHIEST and most prominent citizens had traveled from near and far to mourn the boy king. They had dressed in their most colorful kilts and gowns and golden collars. The vibrant scene looked out of place amid the valley's desolation.

There were so many mourners, and the tomb entrance was so small, that only an elite few were granted the honor of entering it to see where the pharaoh would lie for eternity.

The sarcophagus was heavy, and the stairs were steep, making the journey to Tut's final resting place long and laborious. The sweat from the shoulders of

239

the men made their burden slick, and it was obvious that they were struggling not to drop the pharaoh.

The crowds outside watched anxiously, unprotected from the sun. Even the wealthiest and most delicate women were sweating and miserable, thick eyeliner running down their cheeks. Some were fanned by slaves who provided just a whisper of relief in the still, hot air.

Yet no one dared leave to find a sliver of shade. That would wait until the pharaoh's body was sealed in the ground.

The overseer snuck a glance at the queen. She was radiant in her sorrow, stifling tears; her pain impossible to hide. The overseer had always considered her a fine woman—too young to have endured the loss of two children and a husband. He wondered what would happen to her next and how she would rule this great land.

It was his job to safeguard the tomb's contents, for even the richest and most powerful person in Thebes might be tempted to grab a golden trinket if given the chance. Once the pharaoh's body had been placed in the tomb, the overseer quietly pressed through the crowd and descended the steps. His men were already using wood and plaster to seal the burial chamber.

Tut now lay inside a solid gold coffin, which was nested inside another coffin, which was nested inside another, which was then placed inside a sarcophagus made of yellow quartzite, with a lid of pink granite. The sarcophagus was housed in a burial shrine, which was encased in another, and then another, all of this hidden within the outermost shrine decorated in blue faience and gold.

The structure was so big it filled the burial chamber from wall to wall, with barely an inch to spare.

As the workers labored, gangs of men began carrying Tut's possessions into the much larger room next to the burial chamber. No item of his was considered too small or insignificant—from childhood game boards to travel beds. The work went on for hours, as if Tut were moving everything he owned into a new residence, which, of course, he was.

"We're finished, sir," said the mason, motioning with one hand for the overseer to inspect the work. The plaster was still wet, but it was clear that the job had been expertly done. For a tomb robber to penetrate that chamber would take an act of supreme will—and muscle.

Getting to the pharaoh's body would require knocking down the entire new wall, then disassembling each piece of the elaborate sepulchre.

"You are safe now," murmured the overseer, proud of his handiwork and professionalism. "You were a good pharaoh."

No one would bother the pharaoh ever again.

The overseer was the last man to leave the valley that evening. He mounted his mule and began the familiar trek back to Thebes.

In the distance he could still see the bright royal banners of the queen's procession, and her many servants. He suddenly realized that Tut's tomb was too small — and too well sealed — for her to join him one day.

And yet he knew of no plans to carve a tomb for the queen.

That was odd.

What would become of Ankhesenpaaten?

Chapter 73

Valley of the Kings
November 4, 1922

CARTER WAS SMOKING a cigarette, already his fifth or sixth that day, and was again in a hopeful mood. He sat astride his brown and white mule as it sauntered into the valley, his feet resting in the stirrups of a fine leather saddle.

The dirt path wound between cliffs that climbed steeply, giving way to pale blue sky.

This was the same route Carter had traveled countless times in the past thirty years, and the day seemed like it would be just another day, fraught with expectation but tempered by despair. Before going home the night before he had ordered his foreman to finish clearing the soil down to the bedrock. Now he smoked and wondered how the work was progressing.

Thirty years—A long time for such unpleasant and unrewarding results. No wonder they laughed behind his back in Luxor.

He noticed the valley was quiet.

That could be a problem, for the valley was never quiet during dig season.

His curiosity aroused, and not in a good way, Carter dismounted and tied the animal in the shade. Reis, the foreman, found Carter almost immediately to tell him the news. "I was greeted by the announcement that a step cut into the rock had been discovered," Carter recalled. "This seemed too good to be true, but a short amount of clearing revealed that we were actually in the entrance of a step cut in the rock."

Carter had seen this sort of staircase in many valley tombs, and, he mused, "I almost dared to hope we had found our tomb at last."

Chapter 74

Valley of the Kings
November 4, 1922

HE ORDERED THE MEN to dig. The single step found by the water boy soon revealed more steps, leading deeper and deeper into the hard bedrock a dozen or so feet beneath the entrance to the tomb of Rameses VI.

Carter had worked the valley long enough to know that this was the sort of stairwell associated with tomb construction. The way the rock had been cut was a giveaway.

The men didn't need to be told what to do. All other areas of the job site were abandoned.

As one group dug deeper, clearing away the hard-packed soil and limestone that covered the staircase, another worked up top. Their job was to hack away the soil around the opening to reveal the stairwell's true shape and size.

Carter halted the work at nightfall.

But the frantic pace began again at dawn, with the men back to jabbering.

By the afternoon of November 5, it was clear that they had found some kind of great underground structure. They just needed to dig until an entrance was revealed.

Even with the clang of *turias,* and dust choking the air, Carter's pessimism had returned. He began to ponder the status of the underground chamber.

Was it empty? Had it ever been used? Was it just a storage chamber, or was it actually a burial tomb?

And if it was a tomb, how was it possible that it might have somehow eluded plunder?

The staircase was now a partially covered passageway, measuring ten feet high and six feet wide. Eight steps had been unearthed.

Then nine.

Ten.

Eleven steps.

At step twelve they found the uppermost portion of a door. In his journal, Carter described it as "blocked, plastered, and sealed."

Sealed. That was a positive sign. Carter began to

believe it was possible he had found an unopened tomb.

"Anything, literally anything, might lie beyond that passage," wrote Carter. "It needed all my self-control to keep from breaking down the doorway and investigating then and there."

But he was through investigating—at least for now. As the sun set on the Valley of the Kings November 5, Carter ordered that there be *no more excavation*.

Instead, as much as he wanted to dig deeper, as much as he *needed* to, he ordered the men to fill in the stairwell.

Chapter 75

Luxor
November 23, 1922

AS THE TRAIN FROM CAIRO pulled into Luxor station, nearly three unnerving weeks had passed since the tomb's discovery.

Not a bit of work had been done since the staircase had been filled in November 5. Sentries guarded the site night and day. As added insurance, boulders had been rolled over the opening.

These safeguards were vital. Rumors about the find had already sent droves of tourists into the valley, leading Carter to note wryly in his journal that "news travels fast in the small town that is Egypt."

Yet he refused to open the tomb.

"Lord Carnarvon was in England," he explained. "In fairness to him I had to delay matters until he could come. Accordingly, on the morning of November 6th I sent him the following cable: *'At last have made wonderful discovery in valley; a magnificent tomb with seals intact; recovered same for your arrival; congratulations.'*"

Carnarvon had replied by telegram two days later, saying that he might not be able to come.

Before Carter could take that as a reason to resume digging, a second cable announced that Carnarvon would arrive in two weeks.

"We had thus nearly a fortnight's grace, and we devoted it to making preparations of various kinds, so that when the time of reopening came, we should be able, with the least possible delay, to handle any situation that might arise," Carter wrote.

Somewhat ominously that same week, a cobra had slithered into Carter's home and eaten his pet canary. Otherwise, all went smoothly. A friend named Arthur Callender had been hired, tasked with mundane details Carter might be too busy or too distracted to handle. Lord Carnarvon's favorite foods and drinks were purchased. Electrical wire and lamps were procured in Cairo.

But most of all, Carter spent those two weeks in a state of perpetual self-doubt and second-guessing. It was as if his entire life was tied up in this tomb.

"One thing puzzled me, and that was the smallness

249

of the opening in comparison with the ordinary valley tombs," he wrote. "Could it be the tomb of a noble buried here by royal consent? Was it a royal cache, a hiding place to which a mummy and its equipment had been removed for safety? Or was it actually the tomb of the king for whom I had spent so many years in search?"

As the days slowly passed and the news rapidly spread around the world, Howard Carter became a public figure.

This terrified him. Not that he minded the fame—after years of failure and struggle, it was nice to have his ego massaged. But if the tomb was empty he would be a laughingstock everywhere, and his reputation for failure would only grow.

Carter tried the best he could to go about his business, spending night after sleepless night waiting for Lord Carnarvon and his family to arrive.

At last they were here!

As the train settled to a stop, the dapper earl, wearing a scarf and wool coat on the cool November day, stepped down from his first-class compartment. His daughter Evelyn, a twenty-year-old beauty, was at his side. She and Carter had enjoyed a clandestine enchantment the season before, despite the nearly thirty-year difference in their ages. The two were "very thick" in the words of one chatty observer, though with Carnarvon spending night and day with Carter in Luxor, it was impossible for him to take the romance with Evelyn very far.

Carter greeted them both eagerly, handing Evelyn a bouquet of white flowers. Next, the three would mount donkeys for the six-mile ride to the Valley of the Kings.

The path would take them through the lush green fields outside Luxor. They would then cross the Nile by ferry and continue down the dusty dirt path to the valley.

But even though Lady Evelyn was her usual radiant self, Lord Carnarvon was weak and tired. He needed rest.

The opening of the tomb would have to wait one more day.

A disappointed Howard Carter led his guests to his home, where he would spend yet another sleepless night.

Chapter 76

Valley of the Kings
November 24, 1922

THE FOLLOWING DAY, Carter, along with Lord Carnarvon and Lady Evelyn, arrived at the site. For Carter this had been a thirty-year wait, but even for the Carnarvons the suspense must have been great.

The heavy boulders were rolled away from the tomb. Then Carter's men began clearing the steps.

One group dug away the bits of debris while another swept the steps clean. But this was not as simple as shoveling sand out of a hole, for as they dug deeper and deeper, ancient artifacts mixed with the soil.

Lady Evelyn was beside herself about the historical significance of it all, lovingly studying each new pottery

252

shard or amulet—scarabs, they were called—that turned up in the mountain of dirt.

But Carter's spirits soon plummeted. In his mind these bits of rubble confirmed that he had found not a tomb but a royal trash heap. "The balance of evidence would seem to indicate a cache rather than a tomb," he admitted dourly, "a miscellaneous collection of objects of the Eighteenth Dynasty kings."

The shards were stamped with the names of kings he knew well: Amenhotep the Magnificent, Akhenaten, Tuthmose. Less than pleased with what he was seeing, Carter passed the day looking down from the top step, thinking this might be the end of his career—and an ignominious final chapter at that.

When he was not having such thoughts, he was bent to the ground sifting through whatever new shovelful of dirt the workers had exhumed, now and then admonishing them to be careful. His mood blackened further.

Finally, "by the afternoon of the 24th the whole staircase was clear, sixteen steps in all, and we were able to make inspection of the sealed doorway," he wrote.

He was terribly disappointed by what he saw.

"The tomb was not absolutely intact, as we had hoped," he wrote.

Someone had been there before Carter.

Chapter 77

Valley of the Kings
November 24, 1922

WITH THE DOOR now fully exposed to sunlight and air, there was clear evidence that the plaster seals had been tampered with. A party of tomb robbers—perhaps two—had actually entered the tomb, then had taken the time to *reseal* the door when they had finished ransacking it.

Carter's mind raced in all the wrong directions. Would the break-in have happened in modern times? Impossible. The workmen's huts and loose soil above the bedrock predated the tomb to the time of Rameses VI, at the very least. This meant that whoever rifled through the tomb had done it in a two-hundred-year window between the reign of Akhenaten and Rameses.

There was one thing that gave Carter hope: the seal of Tutankhamen was stamped on the doorway.

This led to more questions: Was the seal evidence that this mysterious king, about whom so little was known, was buried inside? Or was it merely an indication that he had been present or in power when the remains or belongings of others had been relocated to this site? After all, the same seals had been found on the tomb that Davis had once claimed belonged to Tut.

As the light faded and work stopped for the day, the symbol taunted him. Carter's mind kept going back to the same question: *Tut?*

If so, this could be the greatest discovery of modern time.

In the morning Carter would get an answer. At dawn, he planned to be the first man in three thousand years to break down that door.

Chapter 78

Valley of the Kings
November 25, 1922

IT WAS TIME. Well, almost time. Before the door could be destroyed, the royal seals had to be photographed for the historical record.

This singular honor fell to Lord Carnarvon, president of his local camera club back home in England. The earl now stood at the bottom of the narrow stairwell in the pale dawn light, fussing over shutter speeds and apertures.

He was calm and cool as he went about his work—a very professional and dedicated amateur. The last thing

Lord Carnarvon wanted to do was make a mistake that would lead to bad photos — or, worse, no photos at all.

Carter, on the other hand, was beside himself with anxiety. Complicating matters, a much-loathed bureaucrat from the Antiquities Service had arrived to oversee the entry. Rex Engelbach, nicknamed "Trout" by Carter and Carnarvon for his sallow demeanor, was firm in stating that his job title gave him the right to be the first person to enter the tomb.

Carter had never liked Engelbach, with his high-handed arrogance and lack of Egyptology credentials, but on this morning Carter refused to let Engelbach bother him. After a career defined by hard work and failure, Carter was finally about to enter the tomb of Tut. This was no time to be arguing with civil servants. But there was no way that Engelbach was getting into that tomb first. No way in hell.

Carter descended the steps with his sketchbook to draw each of the seals and impressions. These would serve as a backup for Carnarvon's photos, and now the two friends worked side by side at the base of the cramped stairwell.

Carter's sketches were precise in scale and detail. No aspect of the designs went unrecorded.

Only at midmorning, when he had completed the drawings, did Carter trot back up the stairwell with Lord Carnarvon.

It was time.

Carter ordered his workmen to demolish the door.

"On the morning of the 25th," wrote Carter, "we removed the actual blocking of the door; consisting of rough stones carefully built from floor to lintel, and heavily plastered on their outer faces to make the seal impressions."

The crowd gathered atop the steps strained to see what was on the other side. Shadows and debris made it impossible to tell.

Carter descended the steps to have a look. He found himself peering into a long narrow hallway. The smooth floor sloped down into the earth, a descending corridor.

Top to bottom, Carter wrote, the hallway "was filled completely with stone and rubble, probably the chip from its own excavation. This filling, like the doorway, showed distinct signs of more than one opening and re-closing of the tomb, the untouched part consisting of clean white chip mingled with dust; whereas the disturbed part was mainly of dark flint."

How far into the ground the hallway led, it was impossible to know. But one thing was certain: someone else had been there.

"An irregular corner had been cut through the original filling at the upper corner on the left side," noted

Carter. Someone had burrowed through there long ago searching for whatever lay on the other side.

Carnarvon snapped a photograph of the rubble pile. Then a weary Carter gave the order for his men to clear it away, chips and dust and all. Sooner or later the tunnel would have to end.

With any luck, the tomb robbers hadn't taken everything.

Chapter 79

Valley of the Kings
November 26, 1922

IT WAS JUST AFTER LUNCH, which had gone mostly untouched by Carter. He and Lady Evelyn were sifting through a basket of rubble, when a digger ran up the steps with the news: the workers had found a second door.

His heart racing in anticipation, Carter readied himself to go back down the steps to have a look and evaluate the new discovery.

It had been a tumultuous and nerve-racking twenty-four hours for everyone. The diggers had labored into the night, hauling debris out by the basketful. Yet the corridor was still a seemingly endless repository of rubble when they finally quit working.

Making matters worse, the rock was laced with what Carter described as "broken potsherds, jar sealings, alabaster jars, whole and broken, vases of painted pottery, numerous fragments of smaller articles, and water skins"—further signs that this could be an ancient trash heap, *not* a tomb.

Work resumed at first light. Carter and Lady Evelyn carefully sifted through each new basket of debris, searching for historical clues. Carter was an Egyptologist, first and foremost. To him, this diligence was a matter of preserving history. Rather than simply dumping the rubble, as Theodore Davis would have done, Carter meticulously cataloged and recorded each new discovery, however small or seemingly insignificant.

To the anxious onlookers—desperate to see inside the tomb and literally baking in the desert sun—the record keeping was a monotonous waste of time that was slowing things down.

Excitement shot through the crowd as Carter again walked down the steps, now trailed by Lord Carnarvon, Lady Evelyn, and Arthur Callender. The four of them jostled for space with the diggers as they traded places in the slender passage.

Dust filled the air, as did "the fever of suspense."

The second door was an almost exact duplicate of

the previous one. Faint seal impressions were stamped into the surface, bearing the name Tutankhamen.

But this door too had been penetrated in ancient times. The symbol for a royal necropolis was also stamped into the door, and Carter couldn't help being pessimistic. "It was a cache that we were about to open, not a tomb," he wrote.

Still, he stepped forward and began clawing a hole in the upper-left corner of the passageway. His hands trembled as he reached up to pull away thick chunks of plaster and rock.

Callender handed him a long slender iron rod. Grasping it firmly, Carter jammed it into the small opening until it poked clean through to the other side. He tested for further resistance. There was none—no wall of limestone chips or pottery shards, just air.

He had actually broken through to the next level.

Carter had no idea what might happen next, but the great moment had finally arrived. Was it a cache, or was it a tomb? There was only one way to find out. "There lay the sealed doorway, and behind it was the answer to the question," Carter recalled.

He clawed at the hole he had opened with the rod. Then worked with his bare hands, the only digger.

He figured that he deserved as much.

Chapter 80

Tut's Palace
1324 BC

THE EYES GAVE THEM AWAY—always.

So eyes were what Ankhesenpaaten studied whenever a member of the royal court entered her presence
during these dangerous times. As she stood alone in
her study, the morning sun barely brightening the large
stone room, she steeled herself for another day.

If their eyes were slightly downcast, they thought
she had killed her husband. The same was true of those
who fixed strained smiles on their face while avoiding
her gaze.

She could not quite describe the look of those who
believed her. But there weren't many in the palace who

did. It seemed that she had already been tried and found guilty.

"You wanted to see me, Majesty?" said Yuye, her lady-in-waiting. The girl bowed as she entered the queen's quarters, making it hard for Ankhesenpaaten to observe her.

Now that Tut was gone, the entire palace belonged to the queen, but she still kept to her rooms. It felt better that way. Safer. The only change she'd made to palace life was to banish Tut's lover, sending her back to her parents' home with an order never to return to the palace under any circumstances.

"Take a letter," the queen told Yuye. She peered over the girl's shoulder as she spoke, afraid of being overheard or caught at what some would call treason.

Chapter 81

Tut's Palace

1324 BC

YUYE CHEWED ON a fresh reed before dabbing it in an inkwell and pulling out a fresh sheet of papyrus. She was curious as to the content of the letter and was eager to begin.

"My dearest King Suppiluliuma," the queen dictated, her voice unsteady.

Ankhesenpaaten appraised the girl before she continued. If she could trust anyone, it had to be Yuye. Still the queen wasn't sure that sending a letter to the king of the Hittites was a good idea. They were Egypt's enemy, and centuries of battle had bred a powerful distrust between the nations.

But Ankhesenpaaten had a plan, a forward-thinking vision that would benefit Egypt now and in the future. The Hittites were powerful, with a fine army and strong leaders. A marriage between the queen and one of the king's sons could strengthen Egypt for centuries to come.

She continued: "My husband is dead, and I am told that you have grown sons. This is fortuitous for both of us. Send me one of your sons. I will make him my husband, and he will be king of Egypt."

Ankhesenpaaten paused, searching for the proper words to end the letter. All she could do was blurt out the one thought endlessly racing around her brain: "I am afraid for my life."

Yuye looked up at Ankhesenpaaten, uncertain why the queen would say such a thing.

And that is when the queen finally caught a glimpse of Yuye's eyes.

The lady-in-waiting clearly believed that the queen had murdered her husband.

Chapter 82

Tut's Palace
1324 BC

ANKHESENPAATEN HAD BEEN BADLY frightened for exactly twenty-eight days in a row. She had counted each and every one. Now she walked the palace court-yard alone as the sun rose on the twenty-ninth morn-ing after Tut's death.

The sound of water trickling from a nearby fountain gave her a false sense of calm, as did the sparrows flit-ting through the fruit orchard. But she hadn't touched her morning meal and was so nervous that not even a sip of water had passed her lips.

Today would be the day. She was sure of it. But she was certain about nothing else at the palace.

267

It took fourteen days for a messenger to travel from Thebes to the Hittite kingdom. If all went well, a prince would ride to her palace this day and offer his hand in marriage. She would accept, of course. Aye had grown more terrifying with each passing hour, imposing himself upon the palace as the pharaoh. But his claim would never be true if she did not marry him. Once the Hittite prince arrived, the matter would be settled. Aye would once again be a commoner, forced to live out the rest of his days as royal vizier. If that.

Just then she heard heavy footsteps. It was certainly not her lady-in-waiting.

Ankhesenpaaten turned to face Aye.

"Good morning, Highness," he said stiffly. But there was something else in his look. A smugness.

"Vizier."

"What troubles you?" he asked.

She took a calming breath. "That is none of your concern."

While the queen stood, Aye sat on a bench, ignoring proper protocol. That in itself was bold and insulting.

"Stand up," barked the queen.

The vizier smiled, then stood and took a step toward her. "Highness, there is still ample time before your husband's burial. But we must discuss the plan for succession. *Do you have a plan?*"

She said nothing.

"Highness, you need a king beside you to rule Egypt. You must understand that."

"And I will have one," she said.

"There is no one in the land more capable than I—"

"I said I will have one. Please do not discuss this delicate matter with me until my husband has been laid to rest."

They were interrupted by Yuye, whose eyes hastily met those of the vizier. The queen noticed the look that passed between them. Could it be collusion? She pushed the thought aside. Yuye would never betray her. And yet she felt certain something was going on.

"There is a messenger to see you, Highness," Yuye announced.

"Who is it?" demanded Aye.

"That is none of your concern," Ankhesenpaaten said. Her heart was beating wildly. "You are dismissed, Vizier."

A dark-haired man was led into the courtyard after Aye departed. The visitor had left a small retinue behind at the gate. One look told the queen this was not a Hittite prince.

"What is the meaning of this visit?" the queen asked. She looked at Yuye in desperation.

Yuye only shrugged as the Hittite, clearly uncomfortable in the presence of the queen, struggled to explain himself.

"I have a message from my king," said the Hittite. He handed it to the queen, and she read it quickly. Then the Hittite verbalized the message. "Where is the son of the late pharaoh? What has become of him?"

Ankhesenpaaten nearly flew into a rage. "Do you see a male child wandering the palace halls? Do you? Do you see a young prince on a chariot galloping about the grounds? Oh, what I would give for a young boy. Does your king think this is some sort of trick? Did my letter to him seem insincere or unclear?"

The Hittite shuffled his feet and lowered his eyes. "What shall I tell my king?"

"Tell him this: 'Why should I deceive you? I have no son, and my husband is dead. Send me a son of yours, and I will make him king of Egypt.'"

The Hittite stood there not sure what to do next.

"What are you waiting for?" asked the queen. "We are running out of time! We have until my husband is buried, no longer."

As the Hittite fled the palace, Yuye slipped away to find Aye.

The queen stood alone.

Chapter 83

Egyptian Border
1324 BC

THE HITTITE PRINCE'S NAME was Zannanza.

He and his entourage rode fine white horses down the well-traveled dirt road to Egypt. He was pure Hittite by birth, his father's pride and joy. At age twenty-two, Zannanza had already demonstrated courage on the battlefield and shown confidence and diplomatic skill in the royal court. His impending marriage to the queen of Egypt would unify the two nations and make history.

Zannanza would be the new pharaoh and would possess a level of power not even known by his father. The messenger had told the prince that the Egyptian queen was a beautiful young woman. He had described her as "fiery" and "graceful." Zannanza was eager to meet her and take her as his wife.

Now Zannanza drank from a water skin, then passed it to his vizier. "Do you see them?" asked the vizier.

"How could I not," Zannanza replied.

It seemed that the queen had sent a welcoming party. A small band of Egyptians waited at the border, taking refuge from the sun in a verdant oasis. Zannanza imagined they would have something to eat—fruit, perhaps. And fresh water. He had ridden hard all day.

Zannanza and his soldiers and courtiers galloped toward the waiting Egyptians.

As they arrived, a small man with a potbelly trotted forward on his horse to welcome them.

"Greetings. I am Horemheb, the queen's general. She sends her best wishes, Prince."

"I am Zannan—"

The Hittite prince's words ended abruptly. He had not seen the archers behind the tents, nor the arrow racing toward him straight and true that would smack through his forehead. He toppled off his mount, royal blood flooding onto the sand in a massive pool.

His entourage suffered a similar fate. Anyone who escaped the arrows was chased down and hacked to bits by Egyptians wielding swords and axes. As buzzards circled, Horemheb dismounted and walked over to Zannanza.

With his sword, he severed the prince's head and held it high. Horemheb's men cheered and then raced to loot the other bodies.

"For the queen," Horemheb said with a sneer, throwing the head into a bag for its trip back to Thebes.

Chapter 84

Tut's Palace

1324 BC

THE THRONE ROOM WAS DARK and depressing. Ankhesenpaaten and Aye had argued for hours, beginning just after dinner. Now it was midnight, and the queen and the royal vizier spoke by the light of the moon. This same debate had raged for more than a week, and this night the words chosen were no different.

The queen's protestations were heated and loud, unmuffled by draperies and potted plants.

Anyone still awake in the palace could hear her frantic voice, and she knew it.

"Make no mistake: I will rule as king. And you will be my queen," said Aye.

His hands were on his hips as he glared at the stubborn young woman. His sagging neck and paunch made him look more like her grandfather than a man capable of fathering a royal heir.

"I will not do it," she shot back, panic-stricken as he moved closer.

Ankhesenpaaten paced, trying to buy time.

Yuye entered the room, as if on cue.

"What is it?" asked the queen. "Do you have news? Tell me."

Chapter 85

Tut's Palace

1324 BC

AYE BURST OUT LAUGHING. "Yes, she has news. Tell her the news. Tell her the fantastic news about her Hittite prince—who is riding here to save the queen and become pharaoh."

Ankhesenpaaten glared at him. "You knew?"

"Of course I knew." He laughed some more before turning his attention back to Yuye. "Your lady-in-waiting has been a useful spy. Please, Yuye. Tell the queen the news she has so longed to hear."

Shame coursed through Yuye's body, and she couldn't meet the queen's gaze. When she spoke, it was in a low monotone. "The Hittites received your missive,

Majesty. Their king sent a son to Egypt to marry you and serve at your side as king."

"And?" asked Ankhesenpaaten.

"And this prince, whose name was Zannanza, was met at the border by General Horemheb. They had a discussion. Then the prince and his men were slaughtered. A courier galloped here this day with the news—and this."

Yuye placed a leather bag on a table. Aye stepped forward and emptied the contents onto the floor. The prince's severed head hit the tile with a loud thud.

Ankhesenpaaten staggered backward. She could barely breathe as she looked at the head, then faced the vizier.

Aye showed no deference to her now. He mocked her openly. "You are a traitor. I control the priests, I control the money, and I control Horemheb," he declared. "Choose wisely, Majesty. You can either marry me and keep your life, or you can choose to die, just like your husband."

Aye turned and paraded from the room, sandals slapping softly. He took the girl Yuye with him, and that night, to be safe, he made certain she would keep quiet—by slitting her throat. If the lady-in-waiting could betray the queen, she could betray him as well. And the stakes were too high for that.

Chapter 86

Tut's Palace

1324 BC

THE WEDDING RING WAS made of glass and glazed in blue. It had been commissioned to commemorate the important ceremony. Inside the band were inscribed the cartouches of the newlyweds: *Aye and Ankhesenpaaten.*

The queen slipped the ring onto her finger and pretended to be blissfully content. The banquet hall was filled with revelers, and the party would continue well into the night. Bulls had been slaughtered, then roasted over open fires. Beer was served in copious amounts. Try as she might to be a quiet bystander, Ankhesenpaaten was the queen of Egypt. Her every move was being watched, and the country's more illustrious and well-connected residents were curious whether she was truly in love with her new husband.

Hence, the importance of wearing her ring and appearing radiant and happy to all.

She wore a white gown with a floral collar, and eye-liner that showcased her deep brown eyes. Aye stood across the room with Horemheb, looking very much like the old and prosperous pharaoh he now was. He was forty summers older than his teenage bride, and he already had a possessive wife his own age.

How much longer Aye would live was anyone's guess. And then what?

Would Ankhesenpaaten be forced to marry yet again? And who would that be? A foreigner, perhaps?

The only solution, she decided, was to become pregnant with Aye's child. There was no other way to protect herself.

As the party grew louder and more festive, Ankhesenpaaten suddenly felt feverish, clammy. A wave of nausea swept over her. Within seconds she was on her knees, vomiting all over the floor.

Servants rushed to the stricken queen. Aye gazed at her from across the room, his wife Tey now at his side, but he did not go to Ankhesenpaaten's aid.

It was then that the queen locked eyes with her new husband. She saw his look of conceit and triumph and did her best to return it.

When that failed, Ankhesenpaaten waved away the servants and rose unsteadily.

But she crashed to the floor again, this time banging her head and losing consciousness.

The Hittite prince had been carrying a plague virus. That virus had made its way to the queen. That was the story Aye would tell and then record for all history.

A few days later, Ankhesenpaaten was dead. Bowing to his older wife's wishes, Aye refused to bury Ankhesenpaaten in his tomb—or even in Tut's.

Instead, the queen's body was taken downriver and fed to the crocodiles.

Chapter 87

Valley of the Kings
November 26, 1922

CARTER CLAWED AT THE HOLE once again, trying to enlarge it enough to see through to the other side. He was sweaty, winded, and his tobacco-stained fingertips were raw from pulling at the coarse plaster and jagged chunks of rock.

Behind him stood the very attractive Lady Evelyn, along with her father, and Arthur Callender. Farther up the hallway a handful of diggers waited, all hoping for the financial reward that would come if a great discovery was made here today.

Notably absent was Trout Engelbach, the man whose job it was to enter the tomb first. He had left to inspect another dig site several miles away. Carter was supposed to await his return before entering a chamber or tomb. But that was not to be.

When the hole was cleared from the ceiling down to eye level, Carter lit a candle and held it to the opening, checking for foul gases. The candle flickered as air that had been trapped for millennia whooshed from the chamber.

When the flame stopped sputtering, Carter slid the candle through the hole. Next, he pressed his face to the opening, feeling the dust of the centuries against his skin. With one arm inside, holding the candle steady, and his face now looking directly into the chamber, he studied what he could make out in the darkness.

"At first I could see nothing," wrote Carter.

"But presently, as my eyes grew accustomed to the light, details from the room within slowly emerged from the mist. Strange animals, statues and gold—everywhere the glint of gold. For the moment—an eternity it must have been to the others standing by—I was struck dumb with amazement."

"Can you see anything?" Lord Carnarvon asked impatiently, his head close to Carter's ear.

"Yes," Carter responded. "*Wonderful things.*"

Chapter 88

Valley of the Kings
November 26, 1922

"LET ME HAVE A LOOK," the earl demanded. "It's my turn to see. It's my turn now."

Carter not-so-politely ignored him. He had waited too many years for this incredible moment. If anything, it was even better than he could have imagined. He had finally done it! *Wonderful things.*

Carter handed the candle to Callender, exchanging it for a flashlight. He played the beam slowly over the contents of the chamber, spellbound. "Never before in the whole history of excavation," Carter wrote, "had such an amazing sight been seen as the light of the electric torch revealed to us."

This tomb—or cache or whatever it was—did not merely hold a few stray pieces of antiquity. Rather, it overflowed with gold and other priceless treasures.

Carter's eyes now began to distinguish shapes, and he mentally cataloged the amazing contents.

Straight ahead were "three great gilt couches, their sides carved in the form of monstrous animals, curiously attenuated in body, as they had to be to serve their purpose, but with heads of startling realism.

"Next, on the right," he would later write, "two life-sized figures of a king in black facing each other like sentinels, gold kilted, gold sandaled, armed with mace and staff, the protective sacred cobra upon their foreheads."

There was so much more: inlaid baskets, alabaster vases, bouquets of golden flowers and leaves, and a gold and wood throne with a delicately carved inlay.

The room was packed floor to ceiling with furniture, statues, pottery, and all the accoutrements of a wealthy Egyptian.

Then, even as Carter tried desperately to maintain his vigil, he felt a pair of wiry hands yanking him backward, "like a cork from a bottle."

It was Carnarvon.

Planting his feet firmly on the stone floor, the surprisingly powerful earl took hold of Carter's shoulders and finally muscled him aside. The earl was not in good health, so the effort left him breathless.

Yet all was forgotten as he snatched the flashlight from Carter's hand and pressed his nose through the opening.

Once again, Carnarvon was rendered breathless.

Behind Carnarvon stood Carter, slouched against the wall and beaming at Lady Evelyn. Her eyes were riveted on Carter, in awe of the great discovery, but even more, of Carter's passion for his work. Lady Evelyn was one of England's leading debutantes, a woman destined for a life of wealth and status. Howard Carter was many steps beneath her on the social ladder. Yet as she had become her father's companion on trips to Egypt over the previous two years, the attraction between she and Carter had become intense. Lord Carnarvon had taken to keeping a close eye on them.

Only now he wasn't looking. So Carter and Evelyn locked eyes in the dank hallway, "the exhilaration of discovery" bubbling between them. They were struggling to hide their emotions from Callender.

A dazzled Lord Carnarvon finally turned round, gesturing that it was Evelyn's turn to look inside. "Come, come. It's amazing, my dear! You must see for yourself."

Only then did Carter's focus return, allowing him to ask himself the most obvious question: *If this is a tomb, then where is the mummy?*

Chapter 89

Valley of the Kings
November 26, 1922

UNFORTUNATELY, THERE WOULD BE a major problem in looking for the mummy.

The wording of Lord Carnarvon's concession to dig in the valley implied that a tomb's discoverer had the right to enter first. However, as Trout Engelbach had made abundantly clear two days earlier, the Antiquities Service's understanding of the wording was quite different.

Acting under orders from his boss—a Frenchman named Pierre Lacau—Engelbach now demanded that a member of his staff be on hand for the opening of any chamber. The penalty for ignoring that order was severe—Carter and Carnarvon could forfeit much of their claim to the treasure inside.

After all those years of searching, impatience now could mean they'd end up with nothing.

And though Engelbach had left Carter's dig site, he had designated his Egyptian deputy, Ibrahim Effendi, to carry out that task in his absence. But as Carter and his group stood before the second doorway, Effendi too was no longer in the valley. He had returned to Luxor, awaiting news from Carter.

Now Carter and his group were faced with a dilemma: send for Effendi, or break on through to the other side without him.

Carter did both.

Swearing everyone in the tunnel to secrecy, including the Egyptian diggers, Carter wrote a hasty note informing the Antiquities Service of what he'd found. Then he handed the note to one of the diggers and ordered him to wait until nightfall before delivering it.

Next, he again turned his attention to the wall. He enlarged the hole even more.

He was going inside to find the mummy.

Chapter 90

Valley of the Kings
November 26, 1922

LADY EVELYN WAS the smallest of the bunch and was the first to wriggle through the opening. She found herself transfixed by ghostly alabaster vases, and Carter enlarged the hole so the more portly Lord Carnarvon and Arthur Callender could also squeeze through. Then he entered what would become known as the antechamber.

The room was a small rectangle, twelve feet deep by twenty-six feet wide. The ceilings were low to the point of claustrophobia, and the walls unpainted, which was odd, Carter thought. *Why hadn't the chamber been properly finished?*

The Murder of King Tut

The air smelled not just of dust and time but also of perfumes and exotic woods. "The very air you breathe, unchanged through the centuries," marveled Carter.

The group was jumpy now, as if the chamber were haunted.

Carter was surprised to find himself humbled by the timelessness of the moment. There were footprints in the dust from thousands of years earlier, and a container still held the mortar used to build the door. "The blackened lamp, the finger mark upon the freshly painted surface, the farewell garland dropped upon the threshold—you feel it might have been just yesterday," Carter mused.

The four modern-day intruders shone the flashlight about the room, setting aside all historical propriety to hold the golden relics in their bare hands.

Carter opened a small casket painted with images of a pharaoh—*Tut?*—slaying his enemies in battle. Inside were a pair of ancient sandals and a robe festooned with brightly colored beads.

Lady Evelyn gasped with delight as she came across a golden throne with images of a pharaoh and his queen depicted in lapis lazuli. The pair were obviously very much in love, as demonstrated by the tender way the queen seemed to be touching her king.

To Carter's eyes, it was "the most beautiful thing that has ever been found in Egypt."

Outside, darkness fell. The workers and any

remaining spectators had finally left for home. Inside the antechamber, Carter's group continued to revel in discovery after discovery.

But Carter was still not satisfied. A great mystery remained unsolved. He probed the walls, searching for signs of other chambers.

At one point he came upon a tiny hole, and pointed his flashlight through the opening. On the other side lay a very small room, also overflowing with treasure.

There was no sign of a mummy, so Carter resisted the urge to tear down the doorway.

He continued searching, running his hands along the smooth walls, looking for signs of a concealed opening. At last, he found one! On the far right wall, two statues loomed on either side of yet another sealed doorway.

The statues were apparently sentinels, standing guard over the opening, as they had for centuries. "We were but on the threshold of discovery," he would write, still trying to wrap his mind around the stunning evidence. "Behind the guarded door there would be other chambers, possibly a succession of them, and in one of them, beyond a shadow of a doubt, in all his magnificent panoply of death, we shall see the pharaoh lying."

Once again, Carter was faced with the dilemma of whether or not to wait before making a hole in the wall.

Once again, Carter chose to ignore the possible political consequences and see what was on the other side. He only hoped his decision wouldn't prove disastrous at some future time.

But of course, *it would*.

Chapter 91

Valley of the Kings
November 26, 1922

AT THE BOTTOM right corner of the hidden doorway, Carter found a three-foot-tall hole that had been plastered over at some time in antiquity. This was a sign that tomb robbers had preceded him.

For the third time that day, Carter chipped away at some thief's ancient plasterwork, pulled back the stones that had been used to build an impromptu wall, and shone his light through.

At first it didn't look like much. *A narrow hallway?*

Carter slid through ahead of the others. He went feet first, dropping down into a sunken room.

He scanned the narrow walls with his flashlight.

At first it appeared that the light was playing a trick on him.

Then he realized that one of the walls was not a wall at all. He was inside a stunning square chamber, not a narrow hallway.

The low wall that confused him was actually a shrine. It was decorated in blue faience and gold.

He had found the burial chamber.

Chapter 92

Valley of the Kings
November 26, 1922

AS LADY EVELYN and Lord Carnarvon hurried to join him — Callender was too portly to squeeze through — Carter examined the shrine.

He was facing a pair of mighty wooden doors secured with an ebony bolt. Inside, as Carter well knew, would be several smaller shrines like this one. Only after each shrine had been opened would he be able to see the sarcophagus, coffins — and the mummy itself.

At this thought, Carter's heartbeat quickened. *There was definitely a mummy here.* There was no way tomb robbers could have stolen the body without destroying the shrines, and these shrines were in pristine condition.

With Carnarvon's help, Carter slowly and carefully slid back the bolt. The doors swung on their hinges. A linen shroud decorated with gold rosettes was draped over the next shrine. One rosette fell away as the door was opened. Carter slipped it into his pocket without a second thought.

Now he lifted the shroud and saw further evidence that the mummy had not been disturbed: on the bolts of yet another opening, to yet another shrine, was a royal seal. It was the royal necropolis stamp, with a jackal and nine bound captives, *signifying that a pharaoh lay within.*

By now, it was almost morning. The group explored a while longer, but soon they left. The Carnarvons needed rest. They weren't used to the heat or the manual labor. Even Carter needed a break, though for him a short one would suffice.

They climbed the steps, walking from the ancient past—to the cool predawn air of the present in just a few seconds.

Carter's men were still standing guard. They helped secure the tomb for the night and would remain there to protect it from possible invaders.

The greatest day of Howard Carter's life was done.

Chapter 93

Valley of the Kings
December 1922

BACK AT "CASTLE CARTER" — as the news of his discovery sped around the world via cable and telephone — Carter took a moment to think about what he had found and the consequences of that discovery.

The specter of Tut's death hung over Carter as he peered out at the valley from his home's lofty viewpoint. He struggled to make sense of the findings inside the tomb — the toy sailboats, the chariots, the golden shrines and shabtis and jeweled amulets — and wondered how a young man so full of life had come to die. Even more mysterious to Carter: Why was the tomb located where it was? And where was the queen buried?

"Politically we gather that the king's reign and life must have been a singularly uneasy one. It may be that he was the tool of obscure political forces working behind the throne."

Carter couldn't help mentally cataloging the valuable artifacts he had found. He wrote of a "painted wooden casket found in the chamber, its outer face completely covered with gesso." He noted cosmetic jars portraying "bulls, lions, hounds, gazelle, and hare." Most touching, he thought, were "episodes of daily private life of the king and queen." But where was *her* coffin?

He was struck by a painting that depicted Tut accompanied by a pet lion cub and shooting wild duck with bows and arrows, "whilst, at his feet, squats the girlish queen." Another such scene showed the young queen offering Tut "libations, flowers, and collarettes." Still another showed the pharaoh pouring sweet perfume on his queen as they rested together. He had the sense of how young they both were—and how much in love.

Carter was astounded by the gold and jewels found inside the tomb, but he was also stunned by what seemed to be an arsenal.

In the room off the burial chamber, the one with

unpainted walls that Carter referred to as "the treas-
ury," and in the small room off the antechamber
known as "the annex," he had discovered an enormous
stockpile of weapons: thirteen composite bows, three
self bows, and two quivers, one made of linen, and one
of durable leather; two hundred seventy-eight arrows,
many with bronze arrowheads; and an elaborately
carved bow case decorated in gold leaf.

The largest bow suggested that Tut was a man of
some strength, as it was more than six feet in length.

Certainly, Tut was no peaceful king. And just as
certainly, he had a fondness for pursuits other than
archery. The annex also contained throw sticks; several
shields; a leather cuirass that would have been fitted
to protect Tut's chest and shoulders; as well as swords,
boomerangs, clubs, and daggers.

Tut clearly was not his father's son. "The possessor
of the bow could bring down the fleetest of animals
and defend himself against the enemy," Carter noted.

In one corner, lost amid the towering bows of the
hunt and war, was one Tut would have shot as a child.
It was just a foot and a half tall, and its lone arrow was
six inches long.

Carter again found himself wondering about the
circumstances surrounding Tut's death and concluded
that it might not have been an accident. "The sense
of premature loss faintly haunts the tomb. The royal
youth, obviously full of life and capable and enjoying

it, had started, in very early manhood—who knows under what tragic circumstances?—on his last journey from the radiant Egyptian skies into the gloom of that tremendous Underworld," he wrote.

Chapter 94

Valley of the Kings
February 16, 1923

TIME TO OPEN the burial chamber.

Carter had never told Trout Engelbach that he had already entered the chamber, so when the day of the "official" opening arrived, he had to pretend to be curious about what might be inside. And he had to be more convincing now than ever. As news of the great discovery had spread around the world, pandemonium had erupted in Luxor. Suddenly, Howard Carter was a star and a significant historical player.

Beyond that, a certain divisiveness had set in, with Egyptian bureaucrats and foreign hangers-on all trying to get a piece of the action.

"Telegrams poured in from every quarter of the globe. Within a week or two the letters began to follow them, a deluge of correspondence that has persisted ever since," noted Carter.

Letters of congratulations gave way to "offers of assistance; requests for souvenirs—even a few grains of sand from above the tomb would be received so thankfully; fantastic money offers, from moving picture rights to copyrights on fashions of dress; advice on the preservation of antiquities; and the best methods of appeasing evil spirits and elementals."

For a man like Carter, so fond of introspection and relative quiet, things were getting completely out of hand. No one could have predicted this, least of all himself or his detractors in Luxor.

"The Winter Palace is a scream," noted Egyptologist Arthur Mace, whom Carter had recruited to join the excavation party. "No one talks of anything but the tomb; newspaper men swarm, and you daren't say a word without looking around to see if anyone is listening. Some of them are trying to make mischief between Carnarvon and the Department of Antiquities, and all Luxor takes sides one way or the other. Archaeology plus journalism is bad enough, but when you add politics, it becomes a little too much."

An unexpected and rather discouraging problem arose for Carter because of a decision made by Lord Carnarvon. Seeking to make as much money off Tut as possible, the earl signed an exclusive agreement with *The Times* of London that gave the newspaper rights to publish all details of the discovery. This infuriated not only the Egyptian press but also newspapers and magazines from around the world that had been clamoring for a piece of the century's greatest discovery.

Perhaps worst of all, the Antiquities Service and the Egyptian government began trying to take control of the tomb. That would prove to be an ongoing struggle that would plague Carter for years.

And then there was Lady Evelyn. As Lord Carnarvon became more and more suspicious about a relationship between Carter and his daughter, tensions between the men deepened. This, combined with Carter's new fame, drove a wedge between the two longtime partners and friends.

And yet, both men were present as politicians and bureaucrats from Egypt and Britain crowded around the tomb opening. "After lunch we met by appointment, Lacau, Engelbach, Lythgoe, Winlock, and two or three native officials, and we all went in a party to the tomb," recalled the Egyptologist Mace.

Carter led the group of notables inside. The statues in the antechamber had been pushed to the perimeter to safeguard them from haphazard elbows and hips.

A platform had been built along the wall that divided the burial chamber from the rest of the tomb.

It looked very much like a stage, and that day Howard Carter was the star.

He climbed atop the platform, stripped off his jacket and shirt, then placed a chisel blade against the wall.

With a mighty blow of his hammer, Carter began knocking the wall down.

Arthur Mace stood to one side, and as work progressed Carter handed him bits of rock that he had chiseled away. These were in turn handed to Callender, who passed them to a chain of Egyptian workers who collected them, then carried them out of the tomb.

Slowly, the hole widened. After two hours, Carter was "dirty, disheveled and perspiring"—and playing his part perfectly.

Carter squeezed inside and beckoned the others to follow. The alabaster jars, canopic shrine with figures of four guardian goddesses, and spangled shroud were clearly visible now.

The effect on the visitors was profound: they threw their hands up and gasped, dazed by the vision before them. "Anyone coming in would have said we had been taking too much to drink," noted Mace.

Carter could only stand back and watch.

By now he was exhausted, from both the physical labor of opening the hole and the mental exertion of his daily jousting with Carnarvon and the press. He was privately making plans to reseal the tomb and shut himself in his house for a week of quiet and solitude.

When the momentous tour of Tut's burial chamber was over, Carter and Carnarvon said their good-byes. Carter prepared to get down to the hard work of cataloging the tomb's many contents, a job that could take him years but one he couldn't wait to start. He believed it would be the pinnacle of his life's work

Carter and Carnarvon resolved most of their differences before the earl left on February 23. But just six weeks later, Lord Carnarvon was dead. The cause seems to have been septicemia, which arose after he nicked a mosquito bite with his straight razor.

Carter was left to deal with Egyptian politics and bureaucracy on his own. He couldn't do it. Less than a year later, he was evicted from Tut's tomb and from the valley.

One last time, his temperament and stubbornness had done him in.

Chapter 95

Cairo
1931

THE WEDDING RING was made of glass and glazed in blue, and it was still very beautiful. Inside the band were inscribed the names Aye and Ankhesenpaaten.

Ironically, it was Perky Newberry, now sixty-two and a veteran of forty years in Egypt, who turned it over in his hand. He was in Cairo, at the legendary souvenir shop of Englishman Robert Blanchard.

Rather than garish knockoffs of Egyptian tomb relics, Blanchard sold the real thing—purchased from tomb robbers of course.

European tourists were the favored clientele, but Egyptologists sometimes stopped by to see if some new curio had made its way onto the market—a sure sign that tombs were being raided somewhere. Perky already had an extensive collection of amulets and was pecking through the display racks in hopes of adding a new treasure.

He had accidentally stumbled upon the ring, but he immediately understood its significance.

He reread the elaborate inscription to make sure he had the names right before allowing himself a satisfied smile. The ring he held in the palm of his hand solved a mystery that had bothered Howard Carter since Tut's tomb had been opened. Namely, what had happened to Tut's beautiful, young queen?

There had been no mention of Ankhesenpaaten or any other wife on the walls of Tut's tomb. And Aye's tomb, which had originally been intended for Tut, had a painting of his first wife but lacked any indication that he'd taken another.

"Where did you find this one?" asked Perky, trying not to sound excited, lest Blanchard jack up the price to a more exorbitant sum.

"Eastern delta," Blanchard replied with a disinterested shrug.

Perky was careful not to show his surprise.

How had the ring traveled all the way from Thebes, down past Cairo, to the mouth of the Nile? That was odd. Then again, it had been three thousand years. Anything could happen in that time, couldn't it?

Perky went to pay for the ring but discovered that he had forgotten his wallet. He pulled out his pocket notebook and carefully copied the inscription.

Then he placed the ring in the display case and raced to his hotel, intending to hurry back to complete his purchase.

First, he dashed off a quick note to his old friend, who was now back in England.

"My Dear Carter," the letter began. "I have just seen a finger ring at Blanchard's which bears the cartouche of Ankhesenpaaten alongside the prenomen of King Aye. *This can only mean that King Aye had married Ankhesenpaaten, the widow of Tutankhamen.*"

Perky mailed the letter, then hurried back to Blanchard's to buy the ring.

He was too late.

It had just been sold.

Chapter 96

Valley of the Kings
1319 BC

GENERAL HOREMHEB MOURNED his friend and ally, Aye. The two had known each other since they were young men. As Aye was sealed inside the tomb once reserved for Tut, a wave of sadness filled Horemheb's heart. The scar on his face turned a bright crimson.

"How odd," thought Horemheb, "that I can stab a man through the heart and still mourn him."

He scanned the august crowd gathered around Aye's tomb, making eye contact with a few old friends in the process. The tomb was located in a rather obscure spot, far removed from the Valley of the Kings.

Horemheb could understand why Aye would want to be buried there—the location was concealed and remote, which might prevent tomb robbers from finding it. But he also cursed his compatriot for selecting a spot so far from Thebes. The sun was going down, and it was a two-hour journey back to the city in the dark.

Finally, though, he smiled. These were good problems to have. For at the end of the ride, he would not return to his old home or to an army barracks. He would ride triumphantly into the palace.

General Horemheb was now pharaoh.

As the servants collected the plates and wine urns from the final meal, Horemheb picked his way down a rocky trail toward the temporary stable. A long procession of mourners trailed behind him. He could hear the accent of Memphis and Amarna in some of the voices. The high priests led the way.

Despite the death of Aye, the mood today was festive. Perhaps that was on account of the wine or maybe it was because Aye was far from beloved.

Still, Horemheb hoped it would be like this when he died, with celebrants coming from all over Egypt. He loved a good party.

The sun was directly in Horemheb's eyes, but in a moment it would dip behind the rocky plateau ringing the valley. He shielded his face with his hand.

In the distance he could hear the whinny of horses

and knew that his groom was hitching his chargers to the chariot. Horemheb was in a mood to bring the reins down hard on their flanks and race all the way back to Thebes at top speed.

What sort of pharaoh will you be? he asked himself.

Magnificent. Like Amenhotep III.

Yes. I will be magnificent. Let them attach it to my name.

Horemheb instantly knew what he must do next: wipe the slate clean.

Then and there, the fierce general resolved to level Amarna, the city that had been erected by Akhenaten.

The entire city.

All of it.

Gone.

And wherever the names of Tut and Aye were carved on the temple walls, they would be chiseled off. His name alone would remain.

His soldiers would search throughout the land. The job might take years, but the names of Horemheb's predecessors would be obliterated. Pharaohs like Tut would molder in their tombs, edicts undone and commandments overruled. It would be as if Tut and that pretty young wife of his had never existed.

Horemheb was deep in thought as he took hold of the reins to his chariot. Now that he was pharaoh, a procession of bodyguards traveled with him, but he did not acknowledge them. Instead, as he raced down the dusty road back to Thebes, all Horemheb thought of was his plan to erase history.

For more than three thousand years, it had actually worked.

Chapter 97

Palm Beach, Florida
Present Day

I SAT IN MY OFFICE looking out at the view of Lake Worth and the large homes across the water, but my mind was lost in the desert. When I am writing a draft of a book, I occasionally scribble the words *Be There* at the top of a page. This reminds me to make each chapter come alive for the reader, to place myself in the scene. I knew this story was vivid—in my imagination at least. And nothing could be more stunning than what happened to poor Tut in 1925, more than two full years after his tomb was discovered. I could hardly believe it myself.

The investigation would have been impossible

without Howard Carter, of course. It had taken him years just to extract Tut's remains from the burial chamber. The process began the moment the plaster wall separating the anteroom from the burial chamber was knocked down. Reporters clustered outside the tomb and breathlessly awaited news. Doubters in the Egyptology community still believed that Carter had found nothing more than an elaborate closet. And still there was no sign of Tut's mummy.

Poor Carter! And it only got worse for him.

Once his workers had pried the wood apart at the joints and hauled away the protective panels, he was surprised to be looking at another, smaller, shrine.

This too had to be disassembled, piece by piece.

But inside was another shrine. And then another.

In all, there were four shrines, one within the other, like Russian nesting dolls.

Finally, however, Carter reached the sarcophagus. He saw that the lid was made of pink granite and cracked across the center, as if someone had struck it with a hammer or stone club. But who would do such a thing? And for what reason?

At least Carter was fairly certain he had found Tut. The two outer coffins were opened. Politics intruded. Carnarvon died mysteriously. And the Egyptians expelled Carter for a year.

He returned in October 1925 to open the final golden coffin. The mummy was coated with black unguent. When Tut was seen for the first time in modern history, he was covered in black resin and so was *still* cloaked in mystery.

What happened next was as shocking as anything else in the story.

Dr. Douglas Derry of Cairo University was brought in to examine the body. As a professor of anatomy, he was seen as a more suitable choice for this task than Carter. That was debatable. With Tut stuck inside the tomb, Derry got extreme, to say the least. First he tried to chisel Tut out. Then he used hot knives to melt the resin. And then Derry did the unthinkable: *he took a saw and cut Tut's body in half.*

Chapter 98

Tut's Palace
1324 BC

THE SOLDIER, ABDUL, silently tiptoed into Tut's bedroom. He had stood behind a statue as the queen left
her ailing husband, right on schedule. He knew that he
had only a few minutes to do the deed and escape the
palace and then Thebes.

The young pharaoh looked so innocent and helpless
as he lay in his bed, like a child. A sliver of remorse flitted through the soldier's mind but was quickly replaced
with grim resolve and the knowledge that what he was
about to do was for the good of Egypt. The general had
promised him money and a promotion in rank. The

royal vizier had sweetened the deal with a land grant and some cattle.

So the cold-blooded assassin walked to the edge of the pharaoh's bed. He planted his feet wide. Now balanced and stable, he grasped the club with two hands and brought it up high over his head. Though he wasn't tall, he was broad shouldered.

Could it really be this easy to murder a pharaoh? He kept waiting for a guard to spring from hiding or for Tut to rise up and catch him in the act, to forbid his own murder.

The soldier felt the smooth ebony in his hands, and the heft of the stone seemed right for what he was about to do—not so light that it would bounce off the king's head, and not so heavy that it would throw him off balance as he swung.

He was startled as the pharaoh spoke softly in his sleep. "Mother," Tut said.

The soldier put down the club. It wouldn't be right to kill the pharaoh like this. Instead, he placed his strong hands firmly on either side of Tut's windpipe and applied great pressure.

Tut's eyes opened wide. He tried to fight back but was too weak. And then he was dead.

The soldier picked up his club and left the room as quickly and quietly as he'd entered. Later that night, the soldier himself was hacked to death.

Chapter 99

Palm Beach, Florida
Present Day

THE PAINTINGS INSIDE THE TOMB were what told the true story and helped to solve the murder mystery.

On the walls of Tut's tomb are images of Aye peering down at anyone inside the burial chamber. He is shown performing the Opening of the Mouth ceremony and wearing a king's crown. This was the job of the new pharaoh. So not only did Aye perform the task, but he was pharaoh soon enough after Tut's death to commission an artisan to paint his own likeness on the wall of Tut's tomb.

Ironically, these two men, mortal enemies in life,

were now linked for eternity inside this dank chamber. Tut would never be able to escape his tormentor.

My research showed similar paintings on the walls of Aye's tomb. As with Tut's burial chamber, there was an ocher and yellow painting of twelve guardian baboons, representing the twelve hours of the night. There was a painting of Aye hunting in the marshes. Upon Tut's death, Aye was in charge of the wall paintings for the young pharaoh's tomb and, of course, his own.

More important, Aye didn't have Ankhesenpaaten depicted on the walls of Tut's tomb. This was unusual since pharaohs almost always had their favorite wife painted on the tomb walls. Ankhesenpaaten was Tut's favorite and *only* wife. But Aye wanted her all to himself so he could claim the royal throne. His plan was clearly to make Ankhesenpaaten his queen, almost as if Tut had never existed.

So who was responsible for the murder? Who conspired to kill Tut? And why?

They *all* killed him. Remember, the queen actually ruled as pharaoh immediately after Tut's murder. She clearly wanted power—witness her attempt to marry the Hittite prince. That was treason of the most desperate sort. And for what reason? The power to rule Egypt.

All three of them—Ankhesenpaaten, Aye, and Horemheb—succeeded Tut to the throne. Aye double-crossed Ankhesenpaaten by killing the Hittite prince. He was getting on in years, after all, and knew he wouldn't have another shot at the throne. First he murdered the Hittite prince, and then he killed Ankhesenpaaten. The queen had agreed to Tut's murder. No doubt worried that he might die anyway, she believed she could marry her Hittite prince, produce an heir, and continue to sit on the throne.

Ankhesenpaaten had no idea she would be double-crossed by Aye and then murdered.

Nor did Aye know he would be killed by his ally, General Horemheb, who would then succeed him as pharaoh.

Tut was killed by a conspiracy of the three people closest to him in life—Ankhesenpaaten, Aye, and Horemheb. Hundreds of thousands have visited the Tut exhibits, many millions believe they know the story, but few understand the sad tragedy of the boy king.

Case closed.

Today, Tut's mummy resides in a plain wooden tray that Carter had built for him. Investigators over the years have discovered that he had a broken right ankle that seems to have been in a cast; he had suffered a fracture of the right leg that was severe and possibly infected; he even suffered from an impacted wisdom tooth.

But Tut was murdered.

Chapter 100

London
March 2, 1939

HOWARD CARTER DIED ALONE, attended by only a niece who stood to inherit the treasures he had found while toiling more than thirty seasons in the Valley of the Kings.

Four days passed between his death and the burial, long enough for *The Times* to eulogize him as "the great Egyptologist...who gained fame for his part in one of the most successful and exciting episodes in the annals of archaeology."

Now, finally, as sleet threatened South London, Carter was being laid to rest.

Eulogies in *The Times* were a privilege. Usually only

the rich, famous, eccentric, and overachieving were granted the honor.

Carter had once been all four. But the romantic flavor of this eulogy, written by his friend Perky Newberry, belied the fact that Carter's celebrity had long before diminished—and that Perky was his only close friend. In fact, the funeral was embarrassing for its air of sloppiness and apathy: just a handful of mourners gathered around the grave; the birth date etched on Carter's tombstone was off by one year; and, saddest of all, he was buried in a simple hole in the ground.

For a man who had spent a lifetime exploring the elaborate burial tombs of the pharaohs, it seemed a most unfitting way to bid the world adieu.

But there was one saving grace.

Years after breaking off their affair, the one love of Carter's life appeared at the graveside. Lady Evelyn was a small woman, expensively dressed, wearing a broad black hat. Her father had been furious with Carter about their clandestine romance. And when Lord Carnarvon died quite suddenly, just months after the discovery of Tut, she had done "the right thing." Lady Evelyn, daughter of the Fifth Earl of Carnarvon, had turned her back on Carter and found a more socially—and financially—appropriate groom. They were married just months after the public opening of Tut's tomb.

Now Lady Evelyn stood on the spring grass, gazing

at a simple casket and a deep hole in the earth, just as she had once gazed into another burial site while at Carter's side. Maybe that was why she had come. For no matter how far apart Carter and Lady Evelyn drifted, neither could escape the fact that on one glorious November morning, seventeen years earlier, they had been the first people in three thousand years to gaze inside the tomb of a boy king known as Tutankhamen.

Together they had made history and been toasted around the world.

"I see wonderful things," Carter had said breathlessly after his first peek.

Now Carter breathed no more.

The Vicar of Putney closed his prayer book, and Carter was lowered into the ground. Lady Evelyn threw a fistful of earth into the chasm, then walked slowly back to the gravel drive, where her car and driver were waiting.

It was Hodgkin's lymphoma that killed Carter at the age of sixty-four. Tut had died at nineteen, though the cause of his death had mystified Carter right up to the end. It was a mystery that Lady Evelyn had pondered over the years too, a great missing piece of the puzzle of King Tut.

Now in a grave far less noble, Carter slept, never to be disturbed.

Epilogue

Valley of the Kings
1300–500 BC

THE MYSTERY OF KING TUT, the teenage boy king deepened slowly, one sandstorm and deluge at a time.

First, the desert winds whipped tons of sand across the Valley of the Kings, sending the tomb robbers living in caves high above the valley floor to scurry deep inside their homes. The door to Tut's burial chamber was sealed and hadn't been tampered with for hundreds of years.

And as the sand covered the lowest step leading down to the doorway, then another, and another, the doorway had an even better seal.

Now it was entirely buried by rock and grit, hidden from the world.

Rain didn't come to this valley often, but when it did, the water fell with such intensity that massive chunks of earth slid from the walls to the valley floor.

The water turned the sand and limestone into a form of cement, so that anything lying beneath it was encased in a hard rocky crust. In this way, the final steps leading down into Tut's tomb were covered over.

Soon it was as if they had never existed.

Each successive sandstorm and torrential downpour heaped on another layer, until the tomb steps were more than six feet below the surface of the earth. The burial site's location was not just obliterated but forgotten.

Deep below the ground, Tut, the boy king, rested. The walls were sturdy and did not crumble or crack from the new weight above.

Nor did his treasures suffer from rain or humidity— if anything, they were more protected now than they had been before.

Tut lay alone year after year, as if patiently awaiting the day when someone would scrape away all that dirt and limestone—and perhaps unearth the secrets of his life and untimely death.

COMING THIS AUTUMN

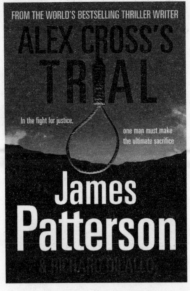

September 2009
Century hardback

October 2009
Arrow paperback

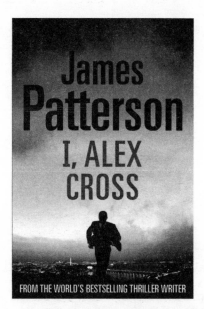

November 2009
Century hardback

A NOVEL WRITTEN BY ALEX CROSS, AVAILABLE FROM
SEPTEMBER 2009

Alex Cross's Trial

James Patterson

Alex Cross writes a story, passed down through his family, of one of the biggest trials in history . . .

Ben Corbett is a brilliant young lawyer in early-twentieth-century Washington DC. Yet he is a disappointment to his wife and father who believe he wastes his talents by doing poor-paying and thankless work helping the poor and downtrodden.

One day, out of the blue, he receives a private invitation to the White House. President Theodore Roosevelt has personally selected Ben to help him investigate rumours of lynchings and a re-emergence of the outlawed Ku Klux Klan in Ben's own hometown of Eudora, Mississippi. Ben accepts the mission handed to him and is given the name of a man in Eudora who will help him in this covert operation – the man's name is Abraham Cross, great-uncle of Alex.

As Ben delves into the murky depths of racial hatred that hide beneath the surface of this seemingly sleepy Southern town, people become suspicious of what he is trying to do, and make it very clear to Ben what he is risking if he continues. Ben must decide if he is willing to lose old friends, his family, maybe even his life for the cause he believes in.

In his quest to bring about justice for the tortured and tormented black community of Eudora, Ben will have to take on the biggest, most difficult, and most dangerous trial of his life. But can one man fight an entire town, an entire state that is stuck in the past and willing to go to any lengths to halt change and the coming of a future that they desperately fear?

Century · London

AVAILABLE IN PAPERBACK FROM OCTOBER 2009

Cross Country

James Patterson

**Alex Cross tracks the scariest killer of them all –
to Africa and back.**

When Detective Alex Cross is called to investigate a massacre-style murder scene, he is shocked to find that one of the victims is an old friend. Angry, grieving, and more determined than ever, Cross begins the hunt for the perpetrators of this vicious crime. He is drawn into a dangerous underworld right in the heart of Washington DC that leads him on a life-threatening journey to the Niger Delta, where heroin dealing, slave trading and corruption are rife.

At the centre of this terrifying world, Cross finds the Tiger – the psychopathic leader of a fearsome gang of killers who are not what they seem. As Cross tracks the elusive Tiger through Africa, he must battle against conspiracy and untold violence.

Alex Cross is in a heart-stopping chase that takes him across a vast and uncompromising landscape and finds him not only hunting for a horrific killer, but also fighting for his own survival.

'[*Cross Country*] opens with one of the most chilling murder scenes I've read in a long time . . . High-octane stuff'
Daily Express

'You're just completely engrossed in it from start to finish. Absolutely incredible . . . The story is unrelentingly exciting.'
BBC Radio 5 Live

arrow books

I, Alex Cross

James Patterson

Alex Cross must battle against the very people he works for to catch a sadistic killer with powerful contacts . . .

Detective Alex Cross is celebrating his birthday when he receives an urgent call from work. An all-too-regular occurrence for Cross. There's been a homicide, nothing new there either. But then comes news Alex wasn't expecting – this time the victim is his niece.

Devastated and grief-stricken, Cross vows to track down the killer. Although, as he investigates he discovers far more than he would wish to know about his niece – she was a high-class prostitute at a very expensive and very exclusive club located just outside of Washington DC. It is clear that this case will test Cross as he never has been before.

As more women working at the same club disappear, it becomes obvious that there is more going on at the sordid mansion than illegal prostitution, and Cross will stop at nothing to solve the mystery of these brutal murders. But he is being foiled at every turn by bureaucracy and a cover-up that stretches as far as the White House. But what are they hiding? And why? Alex can trust no one and will have to do this alone.

$$\overline{C}$$

Century · London

Read on for extracts of

ALEX CROSS'S
TRIAL

A few months after I hunted a vicious killer named The Tiger halfway around the world, I began to think seriously about a book I had been wanting to write for years. I even had the title for it, *Trial*. The previous book I'd written was about the role of forensic psychology in the capture of the serial killer Gary Soneji. *Trial* would be very different, and in some ways, even more terrifying.

In the Cross family, oral history is very much alive, and this is because of my grandmother, Regina Cross, who is known in our household and our neighborhood as Nana Mama. Nana's famous stories include the five decades when she was a teacher in Washington—the difficulties she faced during those years of civil rights turmoil—but also countless tales passed on from times before she was alive.

One of these stories—and it is the one that always stayed with me the most—involved an uncle of hers who was born and lived most of his life in the small town of Eudora, Mississippi. This man, Abraham Cross, was one of the finest baseball players of that era, and once played for the Philadelphia Phaetons. Abraham was grandfather to my cousin, Moody, who was one of the most unforgettable and best-loved characters in our family history.

What I now feel compelled to write about took place in Mississippi during the time that Theodore Roosevelt was President, the early part of the twentieth century. I believe it is a story that helps illuminate why so many black people are angry, hurt, and lost in this country, even today. I also think it is important to keep this story alive for my family, and hopefully, for yours.

The main character is a man my grandmother knew here in Washington, a smart and courageous lawyer named Ben Corbett. It is our good fortune that Corbett kept first-person journals of his incredible experiences, including a trial that took place in Eudora. A few years before he died, Mr. Corbett gave those journals to my cousin Moody. Eventually they wound up in the hands of my grandmother. My suspicion is that what happened in Mississippi was too personal and painful for Corbett to turn into a book. But I have come to believe there has never been a better time for this story to be told.

Alex Cross

THE FIRST TIME I EVER laid eyes on Theodore Roosevelt—God, how he hated the nickname "Teddy"—I was surprised how much he actually resembled the cartoons and caricatures with which the papers regularly mocked him. And now—on this fine summer day in the White House, I saw that the thick spectacles pinching his nose, the wide, solid waist, and the prominent potbelly had only become more pronounced since he took up residence on Pennsylvania Avenue.

Roosevelt jumped up from his desk. He charged across the room toward me, even before his assistant, Mr. Jackson Hensen, could finish his introduction.

"Captain Corbett, a pleasure to you see you again. It's been too long."

"The pleasure is entirely mine, Colonel . . . uhm, Mr. President."

"No, no, no. I'll always prefer Colonel!"

The President waved me over to a green silk sofa near his desk. I sat, trying to contain my excitement at being in the Oval Office, a room that was airy and beautifully appointed, but a good deal smaller than I would have imagined.

A door to the left of the President's desk glided open. In came a tall Negro valet bearing a tea tray, which he placed on a side table. "Shall I pour, sir?"

"Thank you, Harold, I'll do my own pouring."

The valet left the room. Roosevelt went to a cabinet behind his desk, and brought out a crystal decanter. "Except I'll be pouring *this*. What'll it be, Captain, whiskey or wine? I'm having claret myself. I never touch spirituous liquors."

That is how I wound up sitting beside TR on the green sofa, sipping fine Kentucky bourbon from a china teacup embossed with the Presidential Seal.

"I presume our old friend Nate Pryor has given you some idea why I wanted to see you," he said.

I placed my cup on the saucer. "He actually didn't say much, to be honest. Only that it was to do with the South, some kind of mission. A problem with the colored people? Danger, perhaps."

"I've been doing a little checking on you, Ben. It just so happens the place you were born and raised is

339

the perfect place to send you. *Assuming* you agree to this assignment."

"Mississippi?"

"Specifically your hometown. Eudora, isn't it?"

"Sir? I'm not sure I understand. Something urgent *in Eudora*?"

He walked to his desk and returned with a blue leather portfolio, stamped with the Presidential Seal in gold.

"You are aware that the crime of lynching has been increasing at an alarming rate in the South?" he said.

"I've read newspaper stories."

"It's not enough that some people have succeeded in reversing every forward step the Negro race has managed since the War. Now they've taken to the rule of the mob. They run about killing innocent people, and stringing 'em up from the nearest tree."

The President placed the portfolio in my hand.

"These are papers I've been collecting on the situation. Reports of the most horrible occurrences. Some police records. Things it's hard for a Christian man to credit. Especially since the perpetrators of these crimes are men who claim to be Christians."

To be honest, my first thought was that the President was exaggerating the problem. Northerners do that all the time. I hadn't heard of any lynchings in Mississippi since I was a boy.

"They hang men, they hang women, for God's sake they even hang young children," Roosevelt said. "They do the most unspeakable things to their bodies, Ben."

I didn't say a word. How could I? By inference, he was talking about my home town.

"I've tried discussing the matter with several Southern senators. To a man, they claim it's the work of outsiders and a fringe element of white reprobates. But I know damn well it's The Klan, and in some of these towns that includes just about every respectable white man."

"But Colonel," I said, "The Klan was outlawed forty years ago."

"Yes. And apparently now it's stronger than ever. That's why you're here, Captain."

I was glad when Roosevelt reached for the decanter again. This talk of the sins of my fellow Southerners had me upset already, even a little angry.

"Colonel, I haven't spent much time down home since I finished law school," I said cautiously. "But I'd be surprised if there's a problem in Eudora. Folks there generally treat the Negroes well."

When he spoke, his voice was gentle. "Open your eyes, Ben. Since July there have been two men and a fifteen-year-old boy allegedly lynched within a few miles of your home town. It's on the way to becoming a goddamn epidemic, and I—"

"Excuse me, sir. Sorry to interrupt. You said 'allegedly'?"

"Excellent! You're paying attention!" He thwacked

342

my knee with the portfolio. "In this file you'll see letter after letter, report after report from Congressmen, judges, mayors, governors. Nearly every one tells me the lynching reports are greatly exaggerated. There are no lynchings in their towns or districts. The Negro is living in freedom and comfort, and the white Southerner is his boon friend and ally."

I nodded. I didn't want to admit that had I been asked, that would have been very much like my own estimate of the situation.

"But that is not the story I'm hearing from certain men of conscience," he said. "I need to know the truth. I'm glad you don't automatically believe what I'm telling you, Ben. I want a man with an open mind, an honest and skeptical man like yourself who can see all sides of the question. I want you to go down there and investigate, and get to the bottom of this."

"But sir, what is it you want me to find out? Exactly what?"

"Answer these questions for me," he said.

"Are lynchings as common a fact of life as I think they are?

"Is the Ku Klux Klan alive and thriving down there, and if so, who is behind the outrageous resurgence?

"What in hell is the truth—the absolute truth? And what can a President do to stop these awful things from happening?"

He barked these questions at me in the same high, sharp voice I recalled from the parade ground in Havana. His face was flushed red, full of righteous anger and determination.

Then softly he asked, "Will you do it for me, and for this country, Ben?"

I did not hesitate. How could I? "Of course, I am at your service. I'll do what you ask."

"Bully! When can you go?"

"Well, sir, I do have a trial beginning next week in the circuit court," I said.

"Leave the judge's name with Mr. Hensen. We'll take care of it. I want you in Mississippi as soon as possible."

He clapped his hand on my shoulder as he walked me to the door.

From the breast pocket of his jacket he removed a folded scrap of paper, which he handed to me.

"This is the name of a man who will assist you down there. I believe he'll be able to open your eyes to the way your good people of Eudora have been treating their colored citizens."

"Yes, sir." I tucked it away.

"One more thing . . ."

"Sir?"

"I must have secrecy. A cover story has been arranged for you: you're in Mississippi to interview possible Federal judges. If your real mission is exposed, I will deny that I had anything to do with your trip. And Ben, this could be dangerous for you. The Klan murders people—clearly."

In the outer office, I gave the judge's name to Mr. Hensen, then walked down the steps of the North Portico to the curving driveway. To be honest, I hoped for some friend or acquaintance might happen along and witness my emergence from that famous house, but no such luck.

I stepped out onto Pennsylvania Avenue, and turned toward my office. I would have to work late getting everything in order. It seemed I might be gone for a while.

I had just passed the entrance to Willard's Hotel when I remembered the slip of paper the President had given me. I pulled it out, and took a step back to read it in the haze of gaslight from the hotel lobby.

Written in the President's own bold, precise hand were four words:

ABRAHAM CROSS
EUDORA QUARTERS

I thought I knew everybody in Eudora, but I'd never heard of Abraham Cross. "The Quarters" was the Negro section of town. This was the man who was going to teach me about Southerners and lynching?

The fact was . . . I had not been completely honest with Roosevelt. Had he asked me, I would have told him the truth. I already knew more than I cared to know about the horror of lynching.

I had seen one.

James
Patterson

**To find out more about James Patterson
and his bestselling books, go to
www.jamespatterson.co.uk**

I'm proud to support the National Literacy Trust, an independent charity that changes lives through literacy.

Did you know that millions of people in the UK struggle to read and write? This means children are less likely to succeed at school and less likely to develop into confident and happy teenagers. Literacy difficulties will limit their opportunities throughout adult life.

The National Literacy Trust passionately believes that everyone has a right to the reading, writing, speaking and listening skills they need to fulfil their own and, ultimately, the nation's potential.

My own son didn't used to enjoy reading which was why I started writing children's books – reading for pleasure is an essential way to encourage children to pick up a book. The National Literacy Trust is dedicated to delivering exciting initiatives to encourage people to read and to help raise literacy levels. To find out more about the great work that they do visit their website at www.literacytrust.org.uk.

James Patterson